iving The Law of
Attraction and
Enjoying a
Serendipitous Life

Plugging into Source Energy

Kathleen Mackenzie

Outskirts Press, Inc.
Denver, Colorado

Living the Law of Attraction and Enjoying a Serendipitous Life
Plugging Into Source Energy
All Rights Reserved.
Copyright © 2009 Kathleen Mackenzie
V4.0

Outskirts Press, Inc.
http://www.outskirtspress.com

ISBN: 978-1-4327-3658-3

Library of Congress Control Number: 2008940258

Outskirts Press and the "OP" logo are trademarks belonging to Outskirts
Press, Inc.

PRINTED IN THE UNITED STATES OF AMERICA

About This Book

This book is for you if your first desire is spiritual and personal growth. Living the Law of Attraction is not the same as applying the Law of Attraction. The reader of this book should be someone who values and desires to improve upon or find joy, honesty, love, compassion, spirituality and the like – AND someone who also desires to attract abundance and prosperity. The reader should be open to new and old thoughts and be willing to explore life "outside the box."

Do not buy this book if you are an atheist – or if you believe the Christian Bible is simply a collection of stories and that the tales of Jesus have no historical basis. Why? Because I do not want you to waste your money on something that will not resonate with you.

Finally, this book is not for the person who is looking for get-rich short cuts. If financial abundance is your single interest and you find little or no significance in the state of joy and the growth of your spirit – then please save your money and do not buy this book. This is not a step-by-step cookbook or manual with the purpose of promising secret information so you can suddenly become wealthy.

The purpose of this book is to invite you to grow personally and spiritually. The information in it will help you to live deliberately and effortlessly, from your higher self.

This book contains exercises that will help you attract into your life those things you most desire (including financial abundance) – but these exercises must be done using the energy of love, appreciation, and gratitude.

A Message to Everyone

I would like everyone to know that in this book you will read about a variety of topics that are all related to living the Law of Attraction. *Living the Law of Attraction and Enjoying a Serendipitous Life* contains topics such as:

- Effective exercises for manifesting your heart's desires
- How you plug into Source Energy
- Psychics – referrals
- Mediumship and clairvoyance – referrals
- Energy Healing – referrals
- Practical Hypnosis – referrals
- Bible thoughts

- Writers who made a difference in my life
- Manifesting Stories
- Examples of a serendipitous life
- Near-death experiences
- Calling on angels
- Life philosophies
- The Native American Code of Ethics

and more……………..

Living the Law of Attraction is so much more than simply following simple steps to successful manifesting. Living the Law of Attraction is a code of behavior and a way of life.

When you plug into Source Energy, you learn to live in both the physical and the quantum worlds, walking in balance. Living this new life will cause you to "live lucky" in attracting your heart's desires. You will still experience challenges, but you will land on your feet.

This book will introduce you to a way of life that brings together the very old and a very cutting-edge path to success.

New Age folks tend to believe – and are taught to believe - that the Universe exists without care or concern for its creations (us). The predominant belief is that the Universe is impersonal. This New Ager knows and believes otherwise. All our power is rooted in love, compassion and forgiveness. Certainly, our connection to Source Energy is personal, compassionate, electrifyingly genuine, and powerful. Releasing our power by plugging into Source Energy brings our whole self into the picture, not simply our imaginations. The power of our imagination is only one small part of a much larger whole. It is a powerful tool as you assume command of the Law of Attraction in your life – but there is so much more richness, enjoyment, and meaning when you engage the Universe while living a life with purpose and deliberate intent.

Finally, if you have read this far I know that you are a seeker. You seek higher truth and a higher and deeper way of living your life. We, the seekers, are people of love and compassion. It is our responsibility to bring love and compassion into this world. Our country, our states, our cities, towns and neighborhoods, should be about love and compassion. We are children of the Light and that Light will guide our every step as we move forward in this world with loving creation as our constant intention.

You will find that this book resembles a patchwork quilt as I attempt to bring you with me though my journey, the choices that surfaced, the underlying principles of living the Law of Attraction, and the importance of connecting to Source Energy. You will find the power within and your life will never

Table of Contents

A Word Before We Walk i

Chapter 1   Engaging the Universe is Not a 1
             Magic Act
Chapter 2   Balancing Worlds.............................11
Chapter 3   Using the Law of Attraction vs..........21
             Living the Law of Attraction
Chapter 4   My Story 33
Chapter 5   Love is a Choice................................51
Chapter 6   Living Right Now 65
Chapter 7   Back to the Basics, Briefly.................71
Chapter 8   Act "As Though" 77
             Native American Code of Ethics
Chapter 9   Manifesting Exercises.........................91

Chapter 10 Engaging Your Many Resources.......101
Chapter 11 Plugging Into Source Energy 109
Chapter 12 Manifesting Stories 115
Chapter 13 Practical Hypnosis 123
Chapter 14 Energy Healing and Psychics..........127
Chapter 15 Energy Healing 133
Chapter 16 Psychic Readings 141
Chapter 17 Mediumship and Clairvoyance 149
Chapter 18 Answers from My Angels................153
Chapter 19 Near-Death Experience....................165
Chapter 20 VIPs in Our Lives 171
Chapter 21 Lessons from Dag 175
Chapter 22 Challenges and Joys........................183
Chapter 23 Live Deliberately 189
Chapter 24 Goals and Deliberate Creation.........195
Chapter 25 One Confusing Consideration..........203
Chapter 26 Living a Serendipitous Life 209
Chapter 27 In Closing...217

A Word Before We Walk

This book is written as a direct result of the hundreds of email messages I received from readers of my original book, *Not Manifesting? This Book is for You!* Of all those emails, very few readers had experienced any success in manifesting their intentions. The other common thread is that just about every person who contacted me had been educated in the Law of Attraction for years but was not experiencing success in deliberate creation. I thought briefly about sharing excerpts from our emails, with all identities protected, but I couldn't because I consider our email communications personal messages.

Another common thread in the emails is that the

vast majority of them were about manifesting money. Just about everyone who requested advice to manifest financial abundance wanted to get out of debt and reach out to help others. Clearly, the readers who contacted me are really nice people. I felt bad that the majority of these really nice people were feeling like failures and did not understand why they were having such difficulty in working with the Law of Attraction. So many, many people were following the Law of Attraction steps and manifesting nothing but frustration.

Interestingly, another common thread in the emails was the many requests for information and possible referrals for psychics and energy workers. So this book will include thoughts about and referrals for psychics and energy healing.

I am including referrals for services that are available to you no matter where you live. The way I see it, if you have information about the qualities of a reputable psychic (for example) but you have no reputable psychic with whom to connect, the information would be woefully inadequate. I will be referring you to talented professionals who produce results and who do not charge an arm and a leg.

This book is not a rehash of my first book, *Not Manifesting? This Book is for You!* I have read too many books that contained the same information wrapped in different titles and stories. This book you are holding is additional and deeper information. I hope to convey to you the importance of plugging into Source Energy. **You cannot attract high-energy results if you are living a low-energy life. Being plugged into Source Energy will enable you to attract high-energy results. So do not judge your future results by the life you are seeing right now.**

You will read some of my thoughts about the Bible, living a spiritual and spirit-filled life, psychic experiences, energy healing, and more extensive information on practical hypnosis.

Plant a daisy in the desert and celebrate life.
Unknown

Chapter 1
Engaging the Universe is Not a Magic Act

As I said, the vast majority of the hundreds of people who contacted me, regardless of their knowledge of manifesting, were not able to manifest in their own lives. The story was pretty much the same for the people who had studied the Law of Attraction for a decade or longer and for folks who had been involved for only a few months.

I began to explore the possible reasons why my experience with the Law of Attraction is different - because my life is working for me. I knew love and forgiveness had a great deal to do with my success, so in this book I decided to take a linear look at my life, identify the change points, and share my story in the hopes that it will help others. In addition to sharing my journey, I am sharing some spiritual insights, steps to joy and happiness, exercises to help the reader successfully manifest, and some other salient information. Please know that I am NOT a Bible scholar and I don't know the first thing about other holy books. I am simply sharing what has made my life work so well, hoping that readers can take something away from this book and find joy, peace of mind, and successfully manifest their most important desires.

Many of the Law of Attraction teachers say you can be, do, or have anything. And it seems that many teachers are manifesting financial abundance but many of their followers are not. For example, I see that some mainstream religions possess incredible wealth while thousands of people who follow those religions are starving and are being taught to sacrifice. I have seen television evangelists drum up huge dollars with promises of God's forgiveness. I see the followers of the Law of Attraction spending a lot of money hoping to get to that Promised Land. In the events I attended the message was the same. What bothered me were the hundreds of books, DVDs, and CDs that were being sold to the crowds, who were eagerly buying them, hoping to find the answers. Actually, that is why I wrote the first book. I knew my life was working for me and I wanted it to work for the readers as well. BUT, after hundreds of readers contacted me, I know a deeper seriousness in the Law of Attraction movement. Of all the people who contacted me, very few had ever manifested anything and they thought they were alone.

Now, you may be asking yourself if I believe the Law of Attraction movement is phony and the leaders in the movement are just making easy money. Nothing could be further from the truth. **The Law of Attraction is very real and people are genuinely moving from a place of wanting to a place of fulfillment.**

However, the promise of fulfilling financial abundance (and all other desires) simply by focusing, intending, and letting go … well, it's pretty seductive. Have you ever been approached by a carnival barker who was running some kind of game – like pitch and toss, or throwing a ring around some posts, or maybe throwing a baseball at some target? The carnival barker promises that the game is easy and you will certainly walk away a winner with some kind of huge stuffed animal. You may walk away with a huge stuffed animal, but more likely you will walk away with some little ten-cent toy, or maybe nothing at all.

If you use email, you have probably received an email from a Nigerian banker, or a king, asking that you hold a large sum of money in your bank and promising to pay you millions for your help. You probably receive all kinds of email spam inviting you to send money to a lottery in some country and promising you instant wealth. I know I get that email every day! Playing the lottery, taking part in carnival games, and betting on roulette or one-armed bandits (notice they are called "bandits"?) are all seductive. You can actually picture yourself as a lottery winner or you can picture yourself pulling the arm of the bandit while setting off the lights and bells declaring you a winner. It's seductive because it almost begs you to believe that your bills will be instantly paid off, your new house will be fantastic, and your life will be made wonderful, all due to the carnival barker's invitation or the big lottery jackpot.

Yes, people do win and you have to play to win. But bear in mind that in the end, the house always wins (with very few exceptions).

I went to Las Vegas once and spent a few nights at one of the major casinos. I guess I'm just not into gambling because the games did not hold a fascination for me. However, the casino itself was fantastic. It had several floors and the activities seemed endless. There were at least three giant swimming pools with poolside food and beverage service. There were several restaurants in the casino that catered to every taste and pocketbook. There were fancy restaurants and buzz-through buffet lines. There was one entire floor dedicated to the amusement of young children. It offered free rides and cotton candy, and people in animal costumes were constantly entertaining the children. And, of course, there was also shopping galore. There were endless shops on several floors where you could buy anything from a one-dollar bottle of water to a five hundred dollar scarf to a ten thousand-dollar sculpture. And with all of this, you never had to leave the casino!

However, I did leave the casino to check out the rest of the Vegas strip. All the casinos were basically the same. The newest casinos were bigger and glitzier than the ones built just a year before. Each of the casinos had stores, restaurants, entertainment, and, of course, gambling.

I did notice in a big way all the seduction used in the draining of wallets and pocketbooks. The saying is, "People drive into Vegas and walk home." In other words, the house wins. There were instructions on my television set telling me how to refinance my home or how get a home equity loan, right from the casino. There were instructions on how to extend the credit line on my credit cards.

When you walked into the gambling area of the casino and placed a dollar in the slot machine, someone was instantly by your side asking what you'd like to drink. You could ask for beer, wine, or liquor and it would be immediately delivered to you free of charge. If you tipped the server, you could use one of your chips. When you use a purple and white betting chip, it does not feel the same as using an actual dollar bill. I don't know the value of purple chips, but someone told me it could be as much as five hundred dollars!

The pawnshops do a great business on the strip. That is a double-edged sword. You can buy some great stuff in the pawn shops, including beautiful jewelry. But it is so sad when you consider the many people who pawned their jewelry because they felt backed into a financial corner.

Lastly, I do know a couple of people who do well at the casinos. My colleague Linda has been going to Vegas for years. Linda, her husband, and several friends make a yearly trip to Vegas. They have been going for 37 years. They do not even have to pay to stay! Linda has no debt, her house is paid in full, and both she and her husband buy their cars with cash. However, *this is the exception to the rule*. I am very happy for her but she represents the very few who benefit from the lure of the casinos.

I know I've gone on about casinos. I am merely using them as an example of seduction. I'd like to return to Vegas for a short vacation to catch the shows and enjoy the sights and sounds. Reno, Vegas, Fox Woods and the rest of these resorts can be a lot of fun. Just don't fall for the seduction.

Engaging the Universe is Not a Magic Act

So, you may be asking by now what my point is.

My point is, the Law of Attraction is not magic. As far as I know, we cannot manifest a tree, or manifest a lake, or manifest ourselves to be a natural blond if we are, in fact, brunettes. I have never seen anyone use the Law of Attraction to manifest a million dollars. (Although someone may have won Powerball, Megabucks, or a state lottery by now, there are hundreds of thousands of us who practice the Law of Attraction and we are not all lottery winners or casino high rollers.)

However, as we master the Law of Attraction, our intentions are realized more quickly. Overall, the process of deliberate creation takes time. It is true that sometimes our desires appear almost instantly. Sometimes our desires take weeks and months. The reason this is so is that each of us straddles two worlds. We live in this world with the element of time and the frailty of a human body, while we also live in the quantum world, where we are able to move energy particles and create our desires.

Living in this world, where we are bound by time and have fostered a dependence on living from our ego perspective, we challenge ourselves every day to "believe it before we see results," while our ego is screaming at us that what we are trying to do is nuts and to believe only what we already see.

Living the Law of Attraction

Friends and family members may think that we are dreamers or maybe just unrealistic. For that reason, most of us do not share our intentions with people who do not understand the Law of Attraction. You would think that despair is the enemy of hope, but the real enemy of hope is discouragement. Our friends and family members may cause us to feel discouraged if they do not understand the Law of Attraction. Feelings of discouragement that you can absorb from others can cause your attitude of hope and excitement to crash and burn. Despair is far better than discouragement because despair may cause a person to turn to God and seek help. Discouragement may cause a person to become depressed and feel like giving up. The very last thing we need is becoming discouraged because of the actions of the people we love.

As Don Miguel Ruiz writes, "Death is not the biggest fear we have; our biggest fear is taking the risk to be alive – the risk to be alive and express what we really are."

The risk to be alive and express who and what we really are is a challenge for all of us. If we are rejected for who we really are, then where do we go from there?

Who we really are is that spirit inside each of us. When someone dies, we see that person's body in the casket at the wake and funeral. (Each culture has its own rituals for honoring, grieving, and burying the dead. My background is Catholic.) But more often than not, you sense that the body you are watching has nothing to do with the life force of that person.

I was 12 when my dad died on the day after Christmas. On the way back home from the funeral home that snowy night, my older brother explained to me that my dad's dead body was a lot like a junked car. He said that when our car goes to the junkyard, we don't go with the car but that we simply buy another car and drive that one instead. He told me that the body is the vehicle we use to get around and for me not to mistake my dad's body for who he really is.

My brother's explanation made sense to me. It did not lessen the pain of my broken heart, but I knew what he said had to be true because the body in that casket certainly looked like my dad – but that body was simply that, his body. The father I loved was no longer in my life, although his body was left behind.

So, who are we *really*? We are certainly more than a body and all the stuff contained in our bodies. Our bodies really are magnificent. All the systems (circular, cardio, and so on) work together to keep our bodies at the right temperature, our muscles and tendons attached and working, our heart pumping day and night, our eyes seeing, our ears hearing, etc., etc. It's really amazing if you think about it!

Living the Law of Attraction

So, in terms of our bodies, the Universe has given us premium model "cars" in order for us to get around on this earth. But do not be confused. You are so much MORE than your body!

Your power lies in the genuine or authentic you. That authentic you is the you who is using your body temporarily. That authentic you is spirit. You are an extension of God and your genuine self is the part of you that you usually identify as soul or spirit. (Some authors refer to the soul as one's personality – I am referring to your spirit.)

When you awaken your spirit by plugging it back into Source (the Universe, God, etc), your spiritual self will emerge and you will begin to experience life in an entirely new and magical way. It will be the beginning of a new lifetime adventure. It is in this place that learning to manifest your heart's desires will become effortless as you walk down this spiritual road and explore this new world.

Chapter 2
Balancing Worlds

We are learning each day how to balance our two worlds. We came here knowing and accepting the reality of living simultaneously in both the physical world of time and matter and in the nonphysical quantum world of deliberate creation. When we were between lives and deciding what we would learn as we moved forward, we came with a mission – a life purpose. You may have heard the term *old soul*. That is a person who has lived many lives and has learned many life lessons. You sometimes know it when you meet an old soul. You see depth in the eyes and knowledge in him or her. We have agreed to live in a world harnessed to the effects of weather: hurricanes, tsunamis, tornados, blizzards, draught, intense heat, and frigid cold. We have agreed to experience time and the effects the passage of time has on our bodies, as well as on manifesting our desires. We have agreed to grow and to experience our power of deliberate creation through limitation. The limitations or challenges we face could be financial, physical, intellectual, abject poverty experienced in Third-World countries, emotional harm, and so on. We could be born into a very wealthy home and experience a complete lack of love and affection. We could be born into severe poverty but experience being loved deeply and completely. There are endless scenarios of limitations we may experience.

What does that actually mean to us?

When we entered this world we were completely dependent on our parents, or other adults, for our very life. We remained dependent on adults for many years. We acquired from them the lens through which we viewed the world during those years. If we grew up either abused or neglected, we may view the world as a dangerous place. If we grew up loved and protected, we may view the world as a fascinating place. But no matter what our childhood experience, we learned to live in our physical bodies on this physical planet. We learned the lessons of love and loss, joy and pain, winning and losing, living and dying. We learned painful lessons and we learned joyful lessons.

Balancing Worlds

I learned not to trust time when my father suddenly died from a massive heart attack when I was 12 years old. I learned to appreciate the people I love because I had been shown we will not be together long. I also learned that because relationships are not permanent, that loving someone is a choice we make knowing full well there will be loss involved at some time during that relationship. One of the losses I learned over and over again (and continue to learn) is the loss of a dog. You understand before you ever bring a puppy or dog into your home that you will mourn its loss in the end. Pet owners know what I'm talking about.

So we are taxed with lessons of physical existence. This existence includes taking care of our bodies. All of us understand intellectually that smoking cigarettes, excessive alcohol, harmful illegal drugs, excessive food, unhealthy food choices, and lack of exercise all lead to the breaking down of our bodies. We all know better than to do these things, but many of us - with full knowledge of the self-harm involved - make these foolish choices every single day. Amazing, isn't it? I've seen at least one person smoking a cigarette at the same time as having oxygen! It seems that the physical self should be our easiest challenge. Healthy foods and a healthy lifestyle equal a better chance at enjoying this existence with a healthy body. For many of us, though, it's not as easy as it appears. Our challenges are unique to us. We have to accept our challenges and grow from them.

In addition to our physical existence, we have our emotional existence. We learn to love and we learn the loss of love. We fall madly in love and we manage to get dumped, all by the time we reach the age of 14. We marry and we divorce. We have children, bring them up the best we can, and send them on their way - and the phone ringing in the middle of the night always frightens us. How often we ride the emotional roller coaster in life, and how often have we vowed we would never trust another human being again? These emotional roller coasters lead to nights when we get no sleep at all, but then there are nights we fall asleep and stay asleep. When we finally meet the one person with whom we spend the rest of our lives, we realize we are blessed and so happy to be alive…. only to some day say goodbye.

Then we have spiritual lessons to learn. Some of us were brought up going to church or temple or some place of formal worship and learned the faith of our family. Some of us experienced the absence of any particular faith as we grew up and were left to search for faith on our own. As children we may have learned not to take the name of God in vain but also listened to our parents swear at each other during the week. It doesn't take us long to start believing that all religion is hypocrisy. Then again, you may find a religion that tells you exactly how to live and what to believe, with a guarantee of getting to heaven when you die. Religion and spirituality can be very confusing. But we agreed to come here and find our way to the truth.

Lastly, we are responsible for the intellectual side of the coin. It seems to me that the intellectual piece of our existence is both the easiest and the most difficult. On the one hand, we begin learning to tie our shoelaces and we continue to learn for the rest of our earthly lives. We turn to books and life examples. We attended grammar and high school, where we learned to read and write, and were taught smidgeons of history, math, English, the arts, etc. Some of us attended college, where we were challenged to think on our own, and of course to learn socialization skills.

However, at some point, our pursuit of our intellectual potential causes us to fly smack into the face of the quandary of God. We question the very existence of God. We question the validity of the Bible or any holy book. We try to put God in a box and tie a big bow on this God-box because we can finally explain away his existence – until the non-existence of God makes no sense to us either.

Our intellect and our spiritual growth can certainly be at odds with each other and it is uncomfortable to live in that uncertainty – an uncertainty to which we drove ourselves.

Living the Law of Attraction

Then one day we begin the journey of the soul – the journey of the spirit. If you are reading this book, you are on the higher journey of the spirit. When we begin our journey of spirit, we celebrate. We become alive. We have begun to seek the kingdom of God. The reason we live has finally found us.

We learn about quantum physics and realize we can be, do, or have anything. We realize we are here to create. We have stumbled across our destiny and it is exciting. It's just about this time, though, that we forget we also agreed to live in the physical world of time and matter. We get frustrated with our confusion and failure to immediately manifest our desires. We "know" that all we need to do is place our intention, focus, and allow in order to become financially abundant or find our perfect mate, and so on. We forget we agreed to live with limitation.

We need to learn to live freely in our joy of creation *within limitation*. We walk the tightrope of life and we learn to live abundantly, while accepting the reality of this wonderful school we call earth!

Some of us will fall away and give up manifesting our heart's desires. Our intellectual aspect will kick in and convince us that the Law of Attraction is for dreamers and the evidence of our inability to manifest proves this. But, thankfully, most of us know we are dreamers and we know we will learn to manifest our heart's desires, just as we learned to tie our shoes. Living in both worlds has its challenges. We who live the Law of Attraction see our challenges as opportunities to learn and we embrace the adventure!

What is life all about if it is not for adventure? As we uncover our spiritual self, emerging stronger each day, we rejoice. We walk hand in hand with the Law of Attraction as spirit teaches us what it means to set our intention and give ourselves and our intention to the Universe while we wait in joyful anticipation for the Universe to deliver our intention to us - or, of course, to do something even better!

We must also realize that the Universe is not Santa Claus. When we reach for God – Source – the Universe – we become bigger in purpose. We desire to live a more purposeful and loving life as we look for ways to improve our closest connections with Source – the Universe – God. We begin to notice that we are surrounded by all the stuff or the things we have in our lives, to the point, sometimes, of clutter... and yet we ask for more! When we get to the point of recognizing that our wonderful things and our clutter are the result of seeking happiness and fulfillment, we realize that our experience in this world is just the surface of our journey. Our asking will become more spiritual in nature instead of placing our intention on acquiring more things. And the odd events that begin to take place are the surprises the Universe gives to us in the fulfilling of our desires for spiritual growth, as well as for wonderful things for our enjoyment and our abundance!

Many of us learned as children that money is the root of all evil. We are told that the Bible says that money is the root of all evil. Well, that is just not true!! Money is not what is evil. It is the *love of money* that is the root of all evil. The downside to having money is only in the priority we place on it. If acquiring money is more important than your marriage, your health, or your God, then it is time to take a look at your priorities and reassess your life. We have all seen people who were spiritual leaders wind up behind bars due to the love of money.

We must learn to trust the Universe, much as we did when we were children and trusted adults. We may have wanted that second piece of cake and cried when we were not allowed to have it. Or, at 14, we may have been angry when Dad didn't give us the dirt bike we wanted, but we were so happy with our first real motorcycle at age 16 when dad knew we were finally ready to receive our heart's desire. Then there are some of us who begged our parents for permission to drop out of school. This desire may have been because we didn't seem to be succeeding in our classes and were experiencing failure. Or maybe it was because we were being bullied, laughed at, or rejected by our classmates. For some adolescents, school is a very difficult and hurtful experience. In some cases our parents worked with us and supported our efforts and were the reason we graduated from high school. In other cases, our parents understood our cries for relief and allowed us to leave school before graduation. However, if you dropped out of school and now feel discouraged about your future because your life did not work out the way you had hoped, your larger parent, the Universe, is here to support your efforts and deliver opportunities for you to act upon as you claim your success and abundance in this life.

It is really difficult to trust the Universe, but we must. When it seems that we are refused our intention, we must accept that the Universe (like our parents when we were children) knows best and will deliver our heart's desires when we are ready to receive them. It is in this level of trust that we are truly able to let go of the outcome and see our intentions made manifest.

Why? Because we take part in and agree to the decision about the limitations and challenges we will experience in this lifetime. We even take part in and agree to the decisions about who are parents are, what our socioeconomic status is, and where on this earth we will live. So it is reasonable that we take complete responsibility for what we do with our lives and take responsibility for what we do with our power.

Living the Law of Attraction

"It is easy to love the people far away. It is not always easy to love those close to us. It is easier to give a cup of rice to relieve hunger than to relieve the loneliness and pain of someone unloved in our own home. Bring love into your home for this is where our love for each other must start."

Mother Teresa

Chapter 3

Using the Law of Attraction vs.
Living the Law of Attraction

B ecause I am most familiar with the Christian Bible, I will be speaking from that point of view. This does not mean that I believe other holy books are wrong; it simply means that I am most familiar with it.

So here we go.

There is a difference between living the Law of Attraction and using the Law of Attraction. Living the Law of Attraction requires more than going through the intellectual steps of manifesting. It is the act of being. The act of doing falls far short of the act of being, and therein lies the rub.

In the New Testament, Matthew 6:33 tells us that Jesus said to "seek first the kingdom of God, and his righteousness; and all these things shall be added unto you." Matthew 7:7 tells us, "Ask, and it shall be given you; seek and you shall find; knock and it shall be opened unto you; for everyone that asks receives; and he that seeks shall find; and to him that knocks it shall be opened."

So where is the kingdom of heaven? According to the Bible, the kingdom of heaven is in each of us waiting to be awakened. We need first to become aware of the kingdom, to bring it into conscious awareness, and then all that we desire will be made manifest. This is where we learn about our spirit being plugged into Source (the Universe). The flow of life from Source can be compared to the flow of electricity that happens when we plug any appliance into the source of electricity. Acceptance of that flow of electricity is completely our decision: whether or not to flip the switch that turns on the light, turns on the television, the laptop, the iron, etc. We make the decision to plug in and flip the switch that releases our power. Our power to deliberately create, to live our lives at a higher vibration naturally attracting what we desire, is the result of flipping the switch. It causes our power to flow from the Universe to us.

Using vs. Living the Law of Attraction

Seeking financial abundance before seeking the kingdom of heaven, or plugging into Source, is the same as putting the cart before the horse because you have not yet been empowered. Nothing is wrong with financial abundance. Financial abundance is a wonderful thing. Financial abundance delivers freedom on many levels because as financial abundance grows, so do choices – and it is in choices that you realize freedom. If you are solid financially, you can choose to vacation in the places that some people can only dream of going. If you are solid financially, you can afford to buy a home for yourself or your family that some people can only dream of buying. So when you plug into the Universe or Source, you seek the kingdom of heaven first – then everything else falls into place.

I believe that a person does not need to belong to an organized religion, attend meetings, give money, respond to a television evangelist, etc., in order to enter the kingdom of God or to access our higher self. Bringing the kingdom of heaven into consciousness and living a spiritual life does NOT need to be religious or contained within a religion. You do not have to join a church or a group, pay dues, and so on. However, if it is within the community of a church or similar group where you find your spiritual center – then that's absolutely wonderful. I just want the readers to know that membership to any organization is not necessary to seek and find the kingdom of heaven.

Living the Law of Attraction

I remember when I first discovered that Jesus was not a Christian. Embarrassing to say, I was stunned! But there were no Christians in the time of Jesus. Christianity grew from the teachings of the New Testament. In the beginning, the teachings of Jesus were spread by word of mouth. Then, some 40 – 100 years after the death of Jesus, the gospels were written. The gospels were not written by Mathew, Mark, Luke, and John. The gospels were written by anonymous writers who penned the words that had been taught by the original apostles.

Remember, I am NOT a Bible scholar or anything close. However, I find it interesting that in reading Genesis, God created light in the third sentence but created the sun and moon several sentences later. The first light God created and sent into this world must have been spiritual light. Jesus referred to himself as the Light. I believe Jesus was referring to the light found in Genesis. So the Light of God was brought into this world before the light of the sun or the moon. The Christ Consciousness or Spirit of God was given to this world from the very beginning.

Notice that when you read the four gospels, you can't help but notice that the Gospel of John is very different from the others. The other gospels have the apostles finding out all together that Jesus had risen. Jesus came to his apostles and gave them the Holy Spirit. The Gospel of John tells us that only ten of the apostles were together that day. The Gospel of John is the only gospel that did not include Thomas among the apostles who saw Jesus that day and were given the gift and the power of the Holy Spirit. Thomas was present as one of the eleven in the other gospels. In fact, the person who wrote the Gospel of John is the only writer who says that Thomas was a doubter. It tells us that Thomas needed to see proof, needed to place his hands in the wounds of Jesus in order to believe. I have to wonder if the writer of the Gospel of John wanted to leave us with the impression that Thomas was not all that reliable. Now, why on earth would the writer of the Gospel of John desire to leave a less than stellar impression of Thomas?

The Gospel of Thomas was discovered over a half-century ago in the Egyptian desert and apparently dates to the very beginning of the Christian era. It is not accepted by any of the mainstream Christian churches and is said to be Gnostic. The dictionary definition of Gnostic is: "a member of any certain sects among the early Christians who claim to have superior knowledge of spiritual matters, and explain the world as created by powers or agencies arising as emanations from the Godhead." The Gospel of Thomas is not stories or parables but a collection of the sayings of Jesus. Some Bible scholars believe the Gospel of Thomas existed as the first of the gospels. Others believe the Gospel of Thomas was written at the time the Gospel of John was written, decades later. One of the reasons some scholars believe Thomas' gospel was the first one written is exactly because it is a collection of sayings, and it is believed that the writers of the gospels of Mathew, Mark, and Luke drew upon a master list of the sayings and events of Jesus because so many of the words, stories, and sentences are the same. We know the writers did not sit around a kitchen table all writing the gospels together, so it is believed the writers worked off a master list of sorts. So, with all this study of the Gospel of Thomas, we should at least not dismiss it out of hand.

The Gospel of Thomas begins, "These are the secret sayings that the living Jesus spoke and which Didymos Judas Thomas recorded." Both the words *Didymos* and *Thomas* mean "Twin" and are not actually names.

So in the first line, "These are the **secret** sayings that the living Jesus spoke..." the word *secret* implies that these sayings are not for everyone to hear or study. These are the secret teachings that were for only a chosen few. And Thomas wrote them down.

Now let's move forward to the present. We know the Gospel of Thomas was finally found in 1945, one of the Dead Sea scrolls that were sealed in huge vases in the sands of Egypt. The huge difference between the Gospel of John and the Gospel of Thomas

Using vs. Living the Law of Attraction

is in the messages of our spiritual heritage.

The Gospel of John says you can only come to the Father through Jesus and that Jesus is the only begotten son.

Line 50 of the Gospel of Thomas says that we are all children of God and we all share in the same spirit and power. The English translation I am using says: "Jesus said, 'If they say to you, 'Where have you come from?' say to them, 'We have come from the light, from the place where the light came into being by itself, and appeared in their image.' 'If they say to you, 'Who are you?" say, 'We are its children, and we are the chosen of the living father.'"

The Gospels of John and Thomas seem to contradict each other. But if you look back in the gospels, at one point Jesus is teaching his disciples secret truths and those secret truths were teachings the rest of the world was not ready to absorb, to accept, or to learn. Could it be that John was worried about Thomas writing the secret teachings? If that is so, then, according to the Gospel of Thomas, we are children of God and we share the same spirit and power. Thus, our connection to the Universe underscores quantum physics in a very real way. We are all one.

And yes, I am aware that we may never (in this lifetime) know all the answers contained in the holy books, but we all have the responsibility to keep asking salient questions.

Matthew 6:33 (KJV) says, "But seek ye first the kingdom of God, and his righteousness; and all these things shall be added unto you." What does that mean to you?

The only requirement is that we seek the kingdom of God and his righteousness, for no other reason than to seek this kingdom and to know that it is within. We really do need to recognize that we are spirit having a human experience. We need to recognize that a higher self lives within each of us. Our higher self is our genuine self and we need to seek that higher self in order to step into a new life of continuous high vibration as we walk our rediscovered path. When we seek the kingdom of heaven, we are seeking our higher spiritual self. We need to recognize, find, and make manifest our higher self in order to effortlessly live the Law of Attraction.
Pierre Teilhard de Chardin said, "We are not human beings having a spiritual experience; we are spiritual beings having a human experience."

When we truly recognize this fact, we will desire to live the Law of Attraction and to live and walk a spiritual life by loving people and using things instead of loving things and using people. Jesus pretty much sums it up when he tells us to love and forgive. When we seek the kingdom of heaven and ask God to show us the way, we are then empowered to love, forgive, and deliberately create. Once we surrender ourselves to God, we consistently vibrate on a higher frequency and naturally attract similar vibrational creations into our life as we live a life of serendipity. We soon recognize that loving others has nothing to do with the emotions you feel toward your spouse or your family members. You bring love to the world by bringing your higher self to the world.

Many people who are not walking in the kingdom of God are unaware of their greater purpose and feel frustration as they try to "do the right thing" but have no idea of the power of the Universe they could draw upon to help them.

Maybe you see these people at work, where they try so hard but always seem to be beating their heads against the wall because they do not understand nor have they ever thought about their life purpose. They set goals and objectives for their life, and they know in their heart and in their gut they are passionate about their work (or some activity they do in life). But at the same time, they do not feel their lives are making a difference because they feel empty inside or they feel that all the gains they make in their work may not amount to anything in the long run. This emptiness is caused from working from their intellect and sheer force of will, instead of working with their higher power and seeing the pieces simply fall into place (and, of course, not needing to cheat or commit any unethical acts along the way).

People who use the Law of Attraction but are not living in spirit or the kingdom of God have the frustration of setting their intention and allowing the Universe to deliver that intention, but they end up in a seesaw deliberate creation cycle. Sometimes their intention is fulfilled and sometimes it is not, and there doesn't seem to be any rhyme or reason for the lack of consistency. The reason for the inconsistency is this: when a person uses the Law of Attraction but is attracting from a lower self, a lower energy vibration is offered, which usually involves doubt. The person who uses the Law of Attraction but is not attracting through the higher self does not send out that continuous high vibration; thus, the deliberate creations are inconsistent.

Again, as we straddle these two worlds, we tend to live in one world more often than the other, and therein lies the problem.

Without operating from the kingdom of God, which we find within ourselves, we constantly have to "try" to keep vibrations high. We consciously try to feel happy by calling to mind people and situations that make us happy. It can become an effort to be constantly watching our every thought and checking

Using vs. Living the Law of Attraction

on our every emotion. And it can be discouraging to us when we seek counsel as to why we are not as successful as we would like in our deliberate creation, only to be told we need to raise our vibration and let go of the outcome. We end up reducing this inner spiritual power to intellectually following all the right steps without the spiritual power to lead and create.

If you are living like this – constantly checking your thoughts and emotions in order to keep your vibration high and at the same time keeping your intention in front of you while you try to detach from the outcome - then your life of deliberate creation can be stressful and uneven in results.

When you are living the Law of Attraction by discovering and releasing the kingdom of God within, you walk through each day effortlessly, keeping your vibration high because it is just as normal to you as is breathing.

"Figuring out our gifts in life is part of our journey
to becoming enlightened human beings."
Allison DuBois

Chapter 4
My Story

I have been seeking a spiritual life since I can remember. I even liked going to Catholic summer school as a small child so I could hear all the Bible stories. I always knew there was emptiness inside of me and I thought I could find the answers through religion.

I was 12 when my father died from that heart attack on December 26th. My belief in a loving God ended right there. In fact, God was just *dog* spelled backwards for several years after I lost my Dad. During my high school years, whenever the thought came to me to take another look at God, I would turn my back and walk the other way. I did attend a few retreats sponsored by the Catholic Church, but I was only interested in the adventure and some fun, not in finding God in my life. You may be wondering what fun a high school student could have at a retreat. The few retreats I attended had some kind of religious discussions during the afternoons and the evenings were spent playing cards and drinking wine or beer. When I was in high school, the songs that surrounded me described the Kent State killings ("Four Dead in Ohio" by Crosby, Stills, Nash, and Young), the Viet Nam War, free love, and drugs. I loved music and listened to it as often as possible. The Doors were singing "Light my Fire," the Stones were singing about drugs and sex, and of course Dylan was singing, "Everyone must get stoned." Head shops were everywhere and having fun without consequences was the order of the day. I have to say those were wonderful years. Our parents had no clue as to what was going on with that strange generation of ours. Court battles were won in favor of individual rights and freedom. The constitutional rights of high school students did not end when they walked into public school, so boys' hair could hang down below the collars – heck, all the way to the waist!

Looking back, I am sure I selected this time in the evolution of earth to live this life. What an exciting time to have lived! The sixties and seventies was a time of turbulence in this country. It seemed that antiwar protestors were everywhere, in every city and in every town. This was a time of a true test of participatory democracy in our country – and, in spite of the riots and the deaths, democracy won. There were marches on Washington D.C., Martin Luther King Jr. was assassinated, Bobby Kennedy was assassinated, funeral trains ran, black arm bands abounded, crowds were chanting, "Hell no, we won't go!" as a response to the Viet Nam War, and on and on and on. The Moody Blues were always playing in the background of every smoky party. Bumper stickers screamed "Kill 'em all and let God sort 'em out," "Fight Crime – Shoot Back," and… of all things … in the middle of all this turbulence, I would also see bumper stickers that read, "What Would Jesus Do?"

Fast forward to age 23. It was the time of the Catholic Charismatic movement, so being "born again" was in my awareness. It is a LONG story, but here's the short version.

I was walking down the street one summer afternoon and ran into an old friend named David. I was so happy to see him! He was happy to see me and his greeting was, "Praise the Lord." Immediately, I felt bad for him. He was my friend and somehow he had been sucked into this Jesus junk. I expressed my concern and he just smiled with a twinkle in his eye. David was 10 years older than I, so when he asked me to at least listen to him, I did (out of respect for my elders)… and of course, because he was my friend.

Poor David talked to me until he was blue in the face. He quoted Scripture to me and threw some of his own words in as well. He told me I was condemned to hell if I did not become born again. I asked the usual questions. How about people in the far reaches of civilization who never heard about Jesus? Are they condemned to hell? If so, is that fair? So if God is unfair, how do you win? How do you know he won't change the rules, being that he is unfair and all?

Time passed, and David never gave up. Finally, some years later, he asked me if I would go with him, his brother Danny, and a few other friends to a charismatic conference in South Bend, Indiana at the Notre Dame football stadium.

I agreed to go as long as I could drive my own car and take a few of my own friends. My car was a 1966 Oldsmobile 98 that I bought for $50 the day before the trip. I changed the oil myself and filled up the gas tank. The two cars started the trip to South Bend. In New York, my oil light came on. I thought the idiot light was broken because I had just changed the oil. My overriding concern was that the car was overheating and we had to stop several times to pour water into the radiator. Well, soon all the dash lights were on and the engine lost compression and sounded like a million tin cans hitting each other. I was able to coast the car into a Mobil station. The engine compartment was steaming, so the car had to sit for an hour or more. Finally, the mechanic said the oil was empty because the pan screw had been cross-threaded and the oil was slowly dripping out of the pan. He said the engine's pushrods had to look like pretzels and there was no hope for any kind of quick fix. At that point, David and his born-again friends came over to my car and laid hands on the car while asking God to heal it! I now had no doubt that they were all crazy. I knew healings were mind over matter, but a car was just a conglomeration of steel and rubber. However, after 15 minutes of prayer, David instructed me to start up the car. I turned the key and the engine turned over. We filled the gas tank and got underway. I thought (not yet knowing about quantum physics), "Hey God, if you really did fix the engine, how about fixing the radiator? I promise I will have it fixed when I get back home." Well, the engine did not overheat the rest of the way to South Bend and back, until I crossed my town line. Yes, as soon as I got back, the car overheated. I thought to myself that I never should have included that promise in my original thought to God that night driving from the Mobil station in New York.

The conference in South Bend was for the purpose of healing and teaching. We tented on the grounds of the university near the stadium. There was a girl about my age tenting with her family right across from us. She was blind. I went over to speak to her. Her eyes were cloudy-looking and she explained that either she was given too much oxygen at birth or not enough oxygen at birth (I can't remember now). Anyway, she was there to be healed and receive her eyesight. I told her not to get her hopes up. I was not being mean. I was simply being realistic.

I kept a close eye on her at the stadium. There was some man on the field with a microphone praying in tongues (when that happened, I would have loved to flee for my life!) while the thousands of people in the stadium seats were on their feet, arms held high, hands waving in the air. Many of them were singing and just as many were simply repeating, "Praise Jesus." In all of that, I did hear my neighbor say the words, "I can see light." Well, let me tell you, I nearly trampled this little old lady in front of me as I tried to get by her to see the blind girl, who was standing right in front of her. I got to that girl and looked at her eyes. The cloudiness was clearing up right in front of me! She did receive her eyesight. They had her go to a doctor in town to check her eyes. I saw her later and she could see just fine.

You would think I would just give it up and accept Jesus into my heart. Nope. Not me. I was impressed with the experience, but I really didn't know about this Jesus stuff. And, also, fun was always a primary consideration in my decisions. How much fun could a Jesus freak have? Spending my waking hours reading the Bible and going to Bible studies when I wasn't praying in church was not my idea of fun.

A year later, I was playing softball for work. I got up to bat and hit a bad one. I was a place hitter, so when I caught just some of the ball and saw it leave my bat, bouncing once to the pitcher, I hauled off to first base. This was going to be a double play or even a triple, because the bases were loaded. The pitcher threw it to second base for an out. The second baseman threw it to first, but I got there at the same time. The tie goes to the runner so I was safe. But my knee didn't feel so great. I had to leave the game because my knee felt painful and caused me to limp. The next morning when I went to get out of bed, I fell because my leg gave way. A friend gave me a ride to the hospital and x-rays revealed I had broken my kneecap, as well as cracking the femur and breaking some cartilage. They could not operate that day because there was too much swelling due to my 24-hour delay in arriving at the emergency room. There were no open beds anyway, so I was sent home with an air cast (whatever that is) and a pair of crutches. That was on a Thursday. I was scheduled to return for surgery on the following Tuesday.

I decided to play the Jesus card. I called David and told him I needed my knee healed before Tuesday. David and some of his friends came over to my apartment. They laid hands on my leg, prayed in tongues, and told me to have faith and that it would be OK. After they left, I sat there remembering the car being healed (or spiritually fixed) and thought that if that can happen to my car, well certainly it can happen to me.

Tuesday morning came quickly. I came to the hospital as directed. As I was waiting for the doctor to show up, I took my cast off, unwrapped my knee, and began doing semi-deep knee bends. He walked in the door, saw me limbering up, and was astonished. He took additional x-rays "on the house," and to his amazement there was no evidence of a break, no scar tissue, and no bruising. He declared that my knee was healthy and asked me what I had done during the time between visits. I told him about my friends praying for me. He said that prayer certainly didn't hurt.

I could tell you many more stories but I'll fast forward for you.

After a couple of years, I asked Jesus into my heart as my personal Lord and Savior. Actually, this asking occurred when I was walking to a sub shop one night. It was late and I was talking quietly out loud. I said to God that I didn't know if this was all real but I was willing to take the chance, not because I wanted some holy walk or anything remotely religious but because David, who had been badgering me about accepting Jesus, had something I did not have. David had JOY. I knew what it was like to be happy but I wanted to experience that deeper joy inside of me. So I invited Jesus into my heart to be my personal Lord and Savior. Nothing happened. Thunder did not boom and lightning did not flash. But my life did begin to change. The way I saw the world began to change and continued to change as each day unfolded.

Looking back, what I actually did on that night while going to get my steak and cheese grinder was that I finally sought the kingdom of God. Remember, "Seek first the Kingdom of God." So, quite accidentally on my part, I opened myself up to inner acknowledgement of the kingdom of God. I wasn't looking for financial abundance or even a small miracle. I was looking to find the joy that David had. From what I had seen up to that point, that joy could be found only in seeking the kingdom of God within. I knocked on that door and it was opened. Many doors have been opened for me since then.

You might be wondering if I belong to a church or an organized religion or if I spend my days reading the Bible when I am not in church praying. I do not attend a church, nor do I belong to an organized religion. I never did find a church that I thought was both holy and free from condemnation and I don't read the Bible (unless I am looking something up for you). The only times I find myself in church seem to be to attend weddings and funerals. I have never found a church to join because each one I checked out preached some sort of condemnation for someone or someone's lifestyle. Or, on the other hand, I found churches that were embracing everyone but appeared to believe in nothing at all. I found churches that said their way was the only way to heaven and they wanted me to believe exactly as they instructed. Lastly, I found churches that just seemed weird to me. When I was 26, I joined prayer groups, but my efforts did not seem to be leading me in any deeper direction. I remember that I didn't really enjoy fellowship with my prayer group because the people never seemed to have any fun. During prayer group, they prayed. When not in prayer group, all they talked about was the Bible. Now, there is nothing wrong with reading and talking about the Bible. If I found a church where I felt at home, I would certainly attend.

I absolutely wanted the joy, the deeper walk, and the spiritual adventure that comes with this new life. But I also wanted to listen to rock and roll, enjoy roller coasters, and have gin and tonic with a slice of pepperoni pizza on a hot August day.

The Bible says to seek first the kingdom of God and then everything else follows. That is when all else will be added. Matthew 7:7-8 (KJV) says, "Ask, and it shall be given you; seek; and you shall find; knock and it shall be opened unto you. For every

one that asketh receiveth; and he that seeketh fin-
deth; and to him that knocketh it shall be opened."

You are being asked to knock on the door, then to
ask, then to seek, and then the door will be opened.
We are being asked to act. We are being asked to
seek the kingdom of God within.

Does that mean you need to become a born-again
Christian, like in my story? I don't think so. I believe it means that each of us is an extension of God
in that our spirit, the spirit of God, is within each
one of us, and that each of us has the free choice to
seek, find, and give ourselves to our higher self – or
not. How do you give yourself to your higher self if
you don't read or believe the Bible? This is not a
problem, as you will see later on.

Along the way, I developed a burning desire to love
unconditionally, because when I looked around me,
the love I experienced was far from unconditional
(exception given to my mother and father).

Now, understand that unconditional love does not
mean to allow yourself to be treated disrespectfully.
Unconditional love does not require you to endure
negative energy or to live in a potentially dangerous
relationship.

For example, if someone is in a relationship that includes domestic violence, that person needs to find

a way out of that relationship and away from that danger. People stay in domestic violence situations for a number of reasons. Some of them (and they are mostly women) do not believe they have a choice in the matter, or they might even believe they deserve to be abused. Some women stay in that hell for the sake of the children. Some women believe that the abuser will change. After all, he is usually sorry for his brutality, even as the cycle of violence continues. But nowhere in that hell of domestic violence do you find unconditional love. If you are reading this and you are in a domestic violence situation, please seek help. Domestic violence hot lines are set up throughout the country. If you are near a Health and Human Services office or if you have a doctor, seek these folks out. They can help you. If you do not know where to get help and need help to find someone in your area, feel free to send an email to me and I will help you connect with a professional who will be able to help you. You are not someone's punching bag.

Unconditional love meant to me to love without counting the cost and to love even if my love was not returned. I am still today walking that endless road, learning love and forgiveness wherever I am at the moment. The place I work has presented many forgiveness challenges through the years. Remember, in order to learn forgiveness, someone has to do something to hurt you so you can forgive! The lessons can seem fairly brutal and appear to come along all too often. But finding out that living a life where love can win is worth the time and difficulty it takes to get to the pot of gold.

What lesson is your burning desire? What life lesson would you like to learn? Asking yourself this question could indicate part of your life purpose.

I know that I look at the world very differently now than I would have had I not accepted Jesus into my heart so many years ago. My life has been very serendipitous ever since. I had no map to follow, so I happily – and sometimes not so happily – stumbled along.

However, because I did seek the kingdom of God first (again, quite accidentally), my whole self went though a transformation. I took a genuine interest in the gospels, but my interest today is limited to *only* the messages attributed to Jesus. His main theme is love and forgiveness, and to not pass judgment but to recognize the fruits of the trees – meaning, recognize false teachings. Again, I remind the reader I am not a Bible scholar. I am sharing what has meaning for me and what works for me. I genuinely appreciate the roads we all walk, our commonalities and our differences. Judging from my experience, once you are walking in spirit, you are easily able to discern truth from lies. The saying "trust your gut" will come to life. You will also find joy in some of the most unexpected places!

Living the Law of Attraction

Now, moving to the present time: my life is and has been working for me. I know Jesus sits at the table, but I also believe there is room at the table for additional teachers and prophets. I believe there are many roads to the mountaintop. But because I was brought up in an Irish Catholic home, and because I was born into a specific family that practiced specific beliefs, accepting Jesus was an extension of my normal life experience. It was also the beginning of my success in deliberate creation. Someone else may seek first the kingdom of God by looking to Buddha or the teachings of prophets, or Ascended Masters. Not one of us should pass judgment on another's journey. We must leave the judging to the Universe. Although we are all one, we are also all different. When we seek the kingdom of God within, there are many different roads to walk. Seating at the table includes Jesus, Moses, Buddha, and other great and inspired teachers. No single person and no single organized religion can lay claim to having the exclusive rights to God and salvation.

If you would like to seek the kingdom of God within, you can do as I did by inviting Jesus into your heart as your personal Lord and Savior. If that does not resonate with you, ask the Spirit of God within you to be revealed to you and to guide you. By inviting God or the Universe or the Source to live fully in your life, you will live in a higher vibration and you will live that higher vibration each and every day. By living in a state of higher vibration, you will attract those people, events, and things that have a high vibrational frequency. Because you will live in a state of higher vibration, your ability to attract will be as effortless as breathing.

It's true. The love you find by seeking God's kingdom will continue to keep your vibration high and you will attract those higher vibrations into your life. Like seeks like. Please know I am not suggesting that you run around thumping on the Bible. I am talking about walking and living a spiritual life while enjoying this playground and learning environment called earth.

Your life will become all about love. Not necessarily romantic love, but a much deeper love. The love you will unleash from within you is a deep love that walks with you every step of every day and teaches you appreciation for everyone and everything. At some point in this life, you will not be able to walk by a living thing that is in distress without being bothered by the situation. You will find yourself tipping an upside-down bug right-side-up instead of just walking by or, even worse, stomping on it. Your heart will sink if you happen to run over a chipmunk that just dashed in front of your car. Everyone and everything will take on meaning. Your love will continue to expand and your vibration will continue to higher frequencies.

Living the Law of Attraction

I just tipped a beetle upright last week. The poor little guy was struggling on my back porch. I assumed he was dying to be upside down like that but I obviously didn't know that for sure. So I tipped him right-side-up again. He then ambled on his way. I also used the example of the unfortunate chipmunk because I just hit and killed one last month. He ran in front of my car and there was nothing I could do. I saw a very flat chipmunk in my rearview mirror. I felt bad. I feel bad when I see dead deer, chipmunks, porcupines, moose, etc., on the side of the highway when I am going to work or returning from work. The only thing these little guys were trying to do was simply to cross the road.

How many people do you meet who are flattened on the highway of life? All they are trying to do is to cross roads in their lives. When you are living the Law of Attraction, you automatically reach out to help anyone who needs your help. Keep in mind as you reach out that you are walking on a balance beam of sorts. On the one hand, people need a leg up. On the other hand, you do not want to give someone a fish at the expense of that person learning to fish. Do not make another weaker by giving help. Always give out of strength and love. Giving to a local charity may be an answer for you. I support Best Friends in Utah. If you love animals, look up Bestfriends.org to see this special place. Friends of mine have visited there but I have not visited yet. I hope to visit soon. (last week I received a wonderful

My Story

Christmas gift from my lifelong friend, Cyndi Hudson. I received an email from Best Friends saying "Cyndi sent you a gift from Best Friends". She had made a donation in my name to sponsor a homeless animal. Wow, how great is that!)

In addition to supporting Best Friends, I also support the Salvation Army. You need to do what works for you because whenever you support someone or some cause, the world itself is lifted. Bringing blueberry muffins to your elderly neighbor could warm her heart for months to come. If you do not know how to reach out in love, just ask your higher self and your answers will come.

Additionally, as you live the Law of Attraction, you will find yourself being less critical and more loving. You will notice that your depth of understanding and forgiving others and the patience you have with others deepens, and that you are quicker to forgive and to understand.

"I feel that the essence of spiritual practice is your attitude toward others. When you have a pure, sincere motivation, then you have right attitude toward others based on kindness, compassion, love and respect."
Dalai Lama

Chapter 5
Love is a Choice

Every situation provides us with many choices about how to respond. Have you ever been in a grocery checkout line and noticed that someone in the 14-item or less line has a basket full of groceries? And then did you notice the cashier waiting on that person just the same? What did you think?

I used to think, "What a nerve!" I would get so angry that I'd consider leaving my shopping cart right there at the check-out lane and walking out of the store. However, as a matter of practicality, I would invariably wait to pay for my groceries and go home. But I'd scan the parking lot hoping to see the "jerk" who barged into the 14-item or less line with his or her bazillion grocery items. I'd still be thinking about this injustice as I drove home and, of course, I'd have to tell the first person I saw all about my grocery store ordeal. In fact, I'd probably still be thinking about it the next day.

What do I do now? When that happens, and it does not happen often, I will usually grab a magazine off the nearby rack and scan the articles while I wait. Perhaps that person really doesn't know he or she is in an express lane. Perhaps that person thinks he or she is entitled and doesn't care that other people are waiting with the correct amount of groceries. Either way, it just does not matter to me anymore. Whoever those people are, they are loved by someone and are important to someone, and they are important to God. If that person does not realize he or she is in an express lane, who cares? If that person feels entitled to barge into the express lane, who cares? Withhold judgment, wish them well, and read a magazine.

Have you ever experienced poor service or poor food preparation at a restaurant? How did you respond? If the meal is prepared correctly, but the service is poor, I tip less. (By poor service, I mean the server not returning to the table to ask if everything is fine but has the time to chat with the bartender instead.) If the service is great and the food is awful, I return the food to the wait-staff and ask for it to be taken off my bill. When I leave the restaurant, I tip for good service on what would have been the full bill of fare. I just don't let the small stuff bother me anymore.

Have you experienced waiting for an important piece of mail to arrive and not have it arrive on time because there was a mix-up at the post office? No one purposely made a mistake. But, even knowing that mistakes do happen, I would find myself driving to the post office mumbling all kinds of negative words describing the stupidity of the mail sorter. Wow, who on earth did I think I was?

There are so many examples of situations that, in the past, would have sent me over the brink.

Active love is about forgiveness and living above the norm. To live the Law of Attraction, you choose to live above pettiness, greed, hatefulness, selfishness, and unforgiveness. You realize you have many choices about how to respond when someone wrongs you. Choices are delivered to you when you notice the overflowing carriage in the limited item checkout line, or being cut off in traffic, and so on. How often have you given that familiar, universal hand signal to a person who has cut you off in traffic? Living the norm is easy. However, living the Law of Attraction is easier once the ego is checked at the door. The ego gets checked at the door when you surrender yourself to the Universe. However, the ego will keep on fighting to gain ground. But you will have the grace and strength to keep the ego in its rightful and healthy place in your life.

When you are faced with a situation where you really do not know how you should respond, remember the old Jesus bumper sticker. "What would Jesus do?"

How do you respond in love and not be spineless or weird? That would be my first question. You need to remember, this love is very strong. Jesus was no shrinking violet. He turned over the tables in the temple yelling at the money changers. He pretty much told Pilate to jump when he refused to answer his questions, knowing they would finally crucify him. He had lots of patience and very little patience, depending on the situation.

And, when you are faced with a betrayal in your life, and you know you have done nothing wrong, you are not alone. In fact, you are in good company. Jesus broke no law but was put to death anyway. If you are in Orlando, Florida, try to visit the Holy Land Experience. It is across from the Millennium Mall. You could spend a whole day there. There are very good enactments going on all day as you walk through the town of Jerusalem.

One of the fascinating teachings is held in the town square, where one of the staff walks everyone through the arrest and trial of Jesus, noting that Jesus broke no law and was arrested illegally according to Jewish law. He was questioned and beaten but did not answer in the way *he was supposed to answer*. Finally, he was sentenced to death.

Judas Iscariot betrayed Jesus with a kiss. We will all experience betrayal. How do we answer betrayal? We can be angry and miserable for the rest of our lives, never entrusting our hearts to anyone again. Or, when we finally get to the point that we have the choice of letting go and moving on, we do that instead. Living the Law of Attraction enables us to move ahead with our lives, intact and open to life.

When you decide to live deliberately, it is a deliberate life you choose to live. You walk each day living on purpose. You decide the way to see the world. The crowds may want to make these decisions for you by the screaming headlines in the paper or what you hear on the evening news. You decide the way you embrace life. How far are you willing to go to reach happiness and serendipity? Are you willing to live deliberately at a higher vibrational level while living the Law of Attraction?

Some folks have told me they have been so wronged by someone that they cannot forgive. I have met people who were harmed by cheating spouses, best friends, and on and on. They have told me they can't forgive. Well, the cost of unforgiveness is carrying the negative energy in your heart every day and causing your own life to suffer in some way. You can be pretty sure that the person you remain angry with is probably not thinking about you at all. The question is then, is it that you *can't* forgive or that you *won't* forgive? Forgiveness is a choice. Love is a choice. Do what supports your spiritual growth. Forgiving your cheating spouse does not mean to take him or her back into your life. It really means to put yourself first and live a serendipitous life. Withholding forgiveness only hurts you and blocks your flow of energy. Forgiveness is actually putting yourself first because you are acting in love and the result of that act of love is that you do not end up carrying around baggage that blocks the flow of your energy. When you forgive, no matter how hard it is for you to forgive, you will then, through 20/20 hindsight, realize that what you did by enacting forgiveness actually turned out to work in your favor.

When you say you cannot forgive, it's because you are so hurt and so angry that you chose not to forgive. You are hanging onto your hurt and anger because you feel you deserve to do so. Does that make any sense, really? When you hold onto hurt and anger, you are harming yourself. The cheating spouse you divorced is probably happily cheating on someone else and not even thinking about you anyway. Just think of the power those negative emotions hold over you!

Love is a Choice

I am not saying that you should not recognize your hurt and your anger. Allow those feelings to run their course and get rid of them. Perhaps you will be able to get rid of them by using the exercises in this book, or perhaps you would benefit from traditional counseling or hypnotism. Whatever it takes, get healthy and stay healthy for the sake of the person in the mirror.

Another important trait of a person living on purpose is keeping your word. If you say you are going to do something, do it. Do not commit to doing something when, in the back of your mind, you already doubt the integrity of your commitment. Saying "I'll try" is pretty much telling others not to really count on you because you probably won't show up or you will come up with some sort of reason to avoid doing it. So, when you are asked to do something, make a decision before you commit yourself. If you do not want to do whatever it is you are being asked to do, then be adult enough to say no. When we don't live our commitments, we weaken our energy and lower our vibration.

Then, of course, we all make those far-away commitments. These are the commitments you make in June but do not have to do until September. We seem to figure that as long as it is far away, we are fine with it. But have you noticed that as the dreadful commitment date draws near, you begin thinking of ways to try to get out of it? The easiest way is not to make a commitment in the first place.

But suppose you do not want to hurt the feelings of your friend and you *know* your friend will be hurt or angry if you don't agree to whatever it is?

The book *The Velveteen Rabbit* by Margery Williams, with illustrations by William Nicholson, was originally published in 1922. This is a children's story that adults would do well to read. I will share a section of this wonderful book, but please buy it and savor the entire story.

The part I am sharing with you is about the wisdom of the Skin Horse.

"For a long time he [the rabbit] lived in the toy cupboard or on the nursery floor, and no one thought very much about him. He was naturally shy, and being only made of velveteen, some of the more expensive toys quite snubbed him. The mechanical toys were very superior, and looked down upon every one else; they were full of modern ideas, and pretended they were real. The model boat, who had lived through two seasons and lost most of his paint, caught the tone from them and never missed an opportunity of referring to his rigging in technical terms. The Rabbit could not claim to be a model of anything, for he didn't know that real rabbits existed; he thought they were all stuffed with sawdust like himself, and he understood that sawdust was quite out-of-date and should never be mentioned in modern circles. Even Timothy, the jointed wooden lion, who was made by the disabled soldiers, and should have had broader views, put on airs and pretended he was connected with Government. Between them all the poor little Rabbit was made to feel himself very insignificant and commonplace, and the only person who was kind to him at all was the Skin Horse.

The Skin Horse had lived longer in the nursery than any of the others. He was so old that his brown coat was bald in patches and showed the seams underneath, and most of the hairs in his tail had been pulled out to string bead necklaces. He was wise, for he had seen a long succession of mechanical toys arrive to boast and swagger, and by-and-by break their mainsprings and pass away, and he knew that they were only toys, and would never turn into anything else. For nursery magic is very strange and wonderful, and only those playthings that are old and wise and experienced like the Skin Horse understand all about it.

"What is REAL?" asked the Rabbit one day, when they were lying side by side near the nursery fender, before Nana came to tidy the room. "Does it mean having things that buzz inside you and a stick-out handle?"

"Real isn't how you are made," said the Skin Horse.

Living the Law of Attraction

"It's a thing that happens to you. When a child loves you for a long, long time, not just to play with, but REALLY loves you, then you become Real."

"Does it hurt?" asked the Rabbit.

"Sometimes," said the Skin Horse, for he was always truthful. "When you are Real you don't mind being hurt."

"Does it happen all at once, like being wound up," he asked, "or bit by bit?"

"It doesn't happen all at once," said the Skin Horse. "You become. It takes a long time. That's why it doesn't happen often to people who break easily, or have sharp edges, or who have to be carefully kept. Generally, by the time you are Real, most of your hair has been loved off, and your eyes drop out and you get loose in the joints and very shabby. But these things don't matter at all, because once you are Real you can't be ugly, except to people who don't understand."

"I suppose *you* are real?" said the Rabbit. And then he wished he had not said it, for he thought the Skin Horse might be sensitive. But the Skin Horse only smiled.

Love is a Choice

The Skin Horse Tells His Story

"The Boy's Uncle made me Real," he said. "That was a great many years ago; but once you are Real you can't become unreal again. It lasts for always."
The Rabbit sighed. He thought it would be a long time before this magic called Real happened to him. He longed to become Real, to know what it felt like; and yet the idea of growing shabby and losing his eyes and whiskers was rather sad. He wished that he could become it without these uncomfortable things happening to him.

There was a person called Nana who ruled the nursery. Sometimes she took no notice of the playthings lying about, and sometimes, for no reason whatever, she went swooping about like a great wind and hustled them away in cupboards. She called this "tidying up," and the playthings all hated it, especially the tin ones. The Rabbit didn't mind it so much, for wherever he was thrown he came down soft.

One evening, when the Boy was going to bed, he couldn't find the china dog that always slept with him. Nana was in a hurry, and it was too much trouble to hunt for china dogs at bedtime, so she simply looked about her, and seeing that the toy cupboard door stood open, she made a swoop.

"Here," she said, "take your old Bunny! He'll do to sleep with you!" And she dragged the Rabbit out by

61

one ear, and put him into the Boy's arms.

That night, and for many nights after, the Velveteen Rabbit slept in the Boy's bed. At first he found it rather uncomfortable, for the Boy hugged him very tight, and sometimes he rolled over on him, and sometimes he pushed him so far under the pillow that the Rabbit could scarcely breathe. And he missed, too, those long moonlight hours in the nursery, when all the house was silent, and his talks with the Skin Horse. But very soon he grew to like it, for the Boy used to talk to him, and made nice tunnels for him under the bedclothes that he said were like the burrows the real rabbits lived in. And they had splendid games together, in whispers, when Nana had gone away to her supper and left the night-light burning on the mantelpiece. And when the Boy dropped off to sleep, the Rabbit would snuggle down close under his little warm chin and dream, with the Boy's hands clasped close round him all night long.

And so time went on, and the little Rabbit was very happy–so happy that he never noticed how his beautiful velveteen fur was getting shabbier and shabbier, and his tail becoming unsewn, and all the pink rubbed off his nose where the Boy had kissed him."
So, one of the many messages in this wonderful little book is, "You become [real]. It takes a long time. That's why it doesn't happen often to people who break easily, or have sharp edges, or who have

to be carefully kept."

So, if you are carefully selecting your words, cen-
soring yourself, and making promises you do not
want to make, then please understand that the person with whom you feel so uncomfortable is someone who "breaks easily, or has sharp edges, or has
to be carefully kept." Perhaps you will find yourself
reevaluating some of your relationships. If you are
in a relationship with someone who has to be "too
carefully kept," that person is typically easy to anger and quick to criticize. Who needs that? I am not
suggesting you leave the relationship but I am suggesting that you reevaluate it. In order to successfully manifest your desires, you must live in high
vibration. If you are being constantly criticized or if
you are constantly afraid of the person you love,
you need to seek counseling of some kind. Your job
is to be healthy, physically, emotionally, and spiritually.

Chapter 6
Living Right Now

Why is living in the "now" so important? Why is being real or being genuine so important? Many authors tell us to focus our intention on the now and that all affirmations must be done in the now, using the present tense only. When you say, "I am rich right now," and you KNOW you are just getting by paycheck to paycheck, how can you possibly believe you are rich right now? No matter how convincingly you say your intention or affirmation, your brain knows you are not rich. So, what's the point?

The point is this: Whatever you are experiencing today is built on decisions you made leading up to today.

Living the Law of Attraction

For example, I am adjunct faculty for our state university system. I instruct adult classes in human services. I began my adjunct journey teaching college kids. When I taught on a Thursday evening, there were about 20-25 students in my class. When my class fell on a Tuesday evening, there were about 170 students in my class. To make a long story short, it turned out that the students were selecting classes according to their party schedule. The closer the class was scheduled to the weekend, the fewer students signed up for it. Although I got a kick out of the answer to my class-size mystery, I did decide I no longer wanted to teach young people just out of high school.

Soon I was offered a position instructing adult learners. That was in 1993 and I have been adjunct faculty instructing adult learners ever since. My adult students come to class with life experience behind them and a thirst for knowledge. They are footing the cost of their own education and they take their classes seriously. I love being an instructor for the adult student.

I am required to have a master's degree to teach adult learners. It wouldn't matter if I set my intention, did every exercise known to metaphysics, read every metaphysical book, and attended every Law of Attraction lecture. If I did not have a master's degree, I would not have been hired for the position.

Living Right Now

I received my master's degree a few years prior to learning about any of the opportunities to teach. That is what I mean when I tell you that what you experience today is a result of decisions you made in the past.

When did I receive the master's degree? When I did, it was "now." It's in the past, of course, but when I achieved it, it was now. The choices you make now determine your tomorrows – when your tomorrow becomes now.

You cannot go back and change one single decision you made in the past. Your choices remain the same. You could ask someone for forgiveness now, and then tomorrow, your decision to ask for forgiveness will be part of the past. And you cannot leap into the future, either. You cannot bring next week into your now. It will become your "now" when today is in your past.

So, we only live right now. It is currently 9:00 PM Eastern Standard Time. No matter how much I would like to go back to 8:00 PM to experience watching the sun setting again, or to move the clock ahead to 10:00 PM to watch "Boston Legal," I cannot do it. I live now, at 9:02 PM.

So, there is absolutely nothing you can do in the past or in the future. You cannot influence the past minutes or leap to the future minutes. Any behavior or activity on your part that influences your future needs to happen "now." That is why you need to live deliberately each and every day.

The only power you have is right now. So, if you place your affirmations or intentions in the future, the outcomes will always be in the future.

For example, if you say you intend to attract a better-paying job in two months, you are setting your intention in the future and your desire will always be months ahead of you and never come to fruition. *Today* is your only point of power. What you do today will affect your tomorrows.

My mother used to say to me, "If you save pennies, the dollars will take care of themselves." I remember thinking that saving pennies was a very slow way to accumulate dollars – yes, the lesson was lost on me! But, nonetheless, the lesson is true. It is what we do and say today in this moment that influences our tomorrows. That is why we need to place our intentions and desires in the present tense – because, when the Universe delivers our intention, it will then be "now."

In 2003 I decided to get a real estate license. I had no intention of using it right away, but I had the opportunity to act on this idea. I signed up for a six-week course that was held one evening each week. I took the real estate test and passed, by the skin of my teeth. When did I take this course? Now. When did I pass the test? Now. When will I work as a real estate agent in the employment of a real estate broker? No matter when it occurs, it will occur "now." If I do decide to use this real estate license – it is then that I will set my intention, focus my desire, and let go.

"Now" is your only reality in this life of time and matter. The breath you take right now is the only breath that matters.

Do you want your children to have loving and funny stories to share with their children when they are parents? Do you want the memories your children carry to be memories of your love and protection?

If so, live deliberately as a parent every day and choose to love, provide guidance, provide structure, and provide discipline. Let them know every single day that they are always safest in your arms. The memories will take care of themselves.

"When we feel love and kindness towards others, it not only makes others feel loved and cared for, but it helps us also to develop inner happiness and peace. And there are ways in which we can consciously work to develop feelings of love and kindness."
Dalai Lama

Chapter 7
Back to the Basics, Briefly

Before I tell you about a couple of very effective manifesting exercises, I'd like to review the basics, because it's easy to lose sight of the fundamentals.

- It seems that the most difficulty for deliberate creation lies in detachment. Are you detached from the outcome? Do you smile in joyful anticipation of your deliberate creation but at the same time, are truly grateful for the situation you experience today? Are you thinking of ways for the Universe to deliver your intention or are you truly letting go?

Living the Law of Attraction

- Are you sending out mixed messages to the Universe? If you are accidentally sending out mixed messages, the Universe will respond MUCH more slowly than if your messages are confident and given without holding on to even a thread. That is why I use my "magic box." I deposit my intentions and leave them there because I know that if I begin to experience doubt I have shot myself in the foot, so to speak.

- Some years ago I picked up a coin at a New Age store that had on it simply the word *gratitude*. I still have it today. When I place my intention into the box, and I know I am struggling somewhat, I put this coin in my pocket. That way every time I touch it, I remember to give love and gratitude to any areas in my life currently working. Search for "go gratitude" on Google – you may find it interesting. Kathy: Do you mean just "gratitude"?

- Remember Bible passages that support your ability to deliberately create. "The works that I do, ye shall do also; and greater works than these shall ye do" is the one passage that should be just a thought away. It's John 14:12.

- Lastly, do you want others to be as successful as you wish to be? What are you *actively doing* to support the success of others, or perhaps feed the hungry? Tithing is a fine thing to do, but in

72

addition to tithing, to really get supercharged, actively do something, anything. It does not have to be big. Because when we send out un-selfish love, we are given miracles in return. You can do something like showing you value the people you meet during your day – the cash-ier at the grocery store, the person who delivers the mail ¬ by a simple and genuine "Thank you." You might also consider volunteering in your community, even for an hour a month. Your active loving will return to you in spades.

A few more basics..........

Sometimes we hit a wall when trying to manifest IF what we want is not in our best interest. Sometimes we have to walk in darkness to appreciate the joy of the light – and sometimes we learn our best spiritual lessons when we make it through difficult times. But no matter: if we work with the Universe and quantum physics, we get through things more quickly and we realize our experiences are for our best and highest good.

When you place your intention, never use the words "I will" (or similar words) because those words keep your deliberate creation always in the future. And it is fine to aim high when you place your in-tention, but be realistic.

A practice you should be doing already is picturing

your intention the first thing when you get up in the morning and the last thing when you go to bed at night. You should have a picture of your intention taped to your mirror, dresser, or wall to see first thing in the morning each day. If you work using a computer, put a sticky note on the monitor to remind you of your intention. Say your intention is to sell your house. The note should say "house" or "sell house." That way, you stay focused without having to think about it.

Many people use vision boards. A vision board is also called a mind map or a dream board. They are usually pictures on poster board, which you paste deliberately in order to remind you of your deliberate creation intentions. I have seen collages that show the ocean lapping up on the shore with pictures of warm, inviting homes. I have also seen very specific pictures on some boards, like pictures taken in North Carolina. When you create a vision board, you are physically cutting, pasting, and drawing your intention and placing it on tag board or some other surface that you can hang on your bedroom or office wall. You can create a simple vision board by using a sheet of poster board and pasting pictures and words for you to look at each day as you anticipate the Universe delivering opportunities for you so your intention will be made manifest.

A good tool to help you deliberately create is a pamphlet originally published in 1926, by R.H.

Back to the Basics, Briefly

Jarrett. You may be surprised to learn that the notion of deliberate creation is this old, but it is. The pamphlet can be purchased today from online book sellers for a couple of dollars, plus shipping. This work is both very simple and very powerful. It has helped many people as they begin their journey of deliberate creation. It also can help those of us who are advanced in the Law of Attraction but are getting poor to no results because of the complexity of the mud in which we find ourselves stuck some of the time. The more we lead with our heads, using "methods" and 'steps," the more we tend to get stuck in the mire. This powerful book will help you to begin or will help free you from the muck. I used its advice to sell a house not too many years ago.

Many of us have reviewed our habits and have successfully changed self-defeating habits. If you have not done this, you really need to attend to changing bad habits. Habits form from repeated behavior. If you need to change a bad habit, you need to repeat your new behavior until that new behavior is a habit. One self-defeating habit may be a tendency to blame others for your failings or placing blame on yourself for the behavior of others. Another bad habit might be constantly criticizing others for their "stupid ideas" or for other reasons. Have you ever said to someone something like, "What are you? Stupid?" If you take the time to review any bad habits you may have and then make the effort to replace these self-defeating or unloving habits with new

Chapter 8
Act "As Though"

In the many emails I have received, I noticed another common theme. People believed that if they wanted to attract financial abundance, they needed to behave as if they were already financially abundant. However, I was stunned by some examples people shared with me.

Many readers told me that they had "acted as though" they were already financially abundant by giving large sums of money to charity, buying new TVs and other appliances, and buying cars. Some people had even quit their jobs, trusting the Universe to deliver a better one to them. Their reasoning was that if they "acted as though" while trusting the Universe without reservation, then the universal laws would have no choice but to kick in and manifest their intention of financial abundance.

I am sorry to say that based on the email exchanges, the Universe did not make manifest their intentions. The folks I have stayed in contact with had to scramble to find work and some of them had to experience their extravagant purchases being repossessed.

If you are reading this book with the intention of "acting as though" by living outside your financial means, or by placing an intention to be healthy and waiting for good health or a slender or athletic body to be made manifest, or something similar—then please read the rest of this chapter.

It is true that if you would like to manifest financial abundance in your life, you are required to "act as though." But the "acting as though" has to be done with thoughtfulness.

Many million-dollar lottery winners end up in worse shape than they were originally or are flat broke today because they spent money like there was no end to the abundance. They were not ready to handle the sudden influx of wealth. That is not the example you want to follow.

There are the spoiled children of wealthy parents.

Act "As Though"

These celebrities are frequently seen in the news, getting arrested for DUI, going through the sometimes-revolving door of substance rehabilitation, being front-page news for poor behavior and poor choices. These children (regardless of chronological age) live on the surface of life, displaying no depth or appreciation for the opportunities they have been handed. Again, this is not the example you want to follow.

Then there are the wealthy people who display no moral code when dealing with others. These are the people who will stab you in the back for a nickel, who cheat on their taxes, who approve or are involved with criminal behavior, and who in their insufferable selfishness will drive this country into a recession. (Some Wall Street executives come to mind.) Again, this is not the example anyone should follow.

I suppose a person could write an entire book on the irresponsibly or criminally wealthy. Someone probably will write that book – but that person will not be me.

So whose example should we follow when we "act as though"?

We should be following the example of the responsible wealthy. What do the responsible wealthy do, anyway? How did they get to be wealthy? We need to know these things in order to "act as though."

Let's begin with the story of Harland Sanders, who was born in 1890 and passed from this life in 1980. You may know him better as Colonel Sanders of Kentucky Fried Chicken fame.

This wealthy man was only five years old when his father died. Harland dropped out of school—and it wasn't high school. This boy dropped out of school when he was only seven years old. His life went from difficult to horrible when he had to endure beatings from his stepfather. It got to the point that he had to run away from home. As a runaway, Harland worked any job he could find and was going absolutely nowhere but in a large circle of failure. Finally, at age 16, he joined the Army.

Later, Harland was able to open a small gas station. That is where he cooked his own chicken dishes and sold them to people who stopped by for gas and small repairs. People began talking about Harland's food and how tasty it was. People began going to the gas station for chicken instead of or in addition to gas. He began serving them at his own kitchen table and any available seats. Finally, he began selling complete dinners to travelers so they could take them home and serve them there. He called his idea "Sunday Dinner Seven Days a Week."

Harland then got work as a chef in a local restaurant, where he worked for almost a decade as he dedicated himself to creating the perfect chicken dish. He learned different ways to cook his chicken: frying, using a pressure cooker, using the oven, etc.

Then, in the 1950s, a new interstate highway, Highway 75, was planned and it was designed to bypass Corbin, Kentucky, the home of Harland's restaurant business. The value of his restaurant fell because of this proposed interstate. Harland sold his restaurant operations and, after paying his bills, was just about flat broke. He was in his early 60s at the time, and living on his Social Security check of $105 monthly.

However, he did not give up in discouragement, but instead decided to chase his dream. He pursued franchising his now-famous fried chicken. He cooked batches of his chicken for restaurant owners all over the country. If the owner liked his chicken, Harland entered into an agreement that would pay him .05 cents for each of his chicken dinners the restaurant sold. By 1963 there were more than 600 franchises operating. By 1964, Harland Sanders sold his interest in his U.S. company for two million dollars and continued to collect franchise fees for his Canadian franchises.

At that point, it seemed that Colonel Harland Sanders could easily purchase anything his heart desired. If he were here today, his desires might be a 60" plasma or LDC television with surround sound, all contained in a special entertainment room located in a lavish home where he could spend his days watching movies and eating popcorn. (These are examples. I have no idea if Harland Sanders even liked movies or popcorn.)

But instead of resting in his wealth, he used it to create charitable organizations that created scholarships. Today, his trusts are responsible for generous donations to health care groups. In fact, they are responsible for creating a wing of the Trillium Health Care Center in Canada, which is focused on women and children's health care. That wing is actually named after him.

Colonel Sanders was a very generous man. He was poor through childhood and he had to run away from home to escape beatings. Later, just when things seemed to be going his way, when he was chef at the restaurant, fate seemed to pull the rug out from under him. What did he do? He kept believing in his dream and kept going until he attained success. When he was successful, he gave to the community and through his trusts; he keeps giving to the community.

When Colonel Sanders was 90 years old, he was diagnosed with leukemia and died from that disease. He is gone, but look at his legacy! He is a man for every person to respect – and to use as an example of the "responsible wealthy."

Perhaps you would like to be like Brad Pitt, Harland Sanders, Walt Disney or someone else who appears to have financial abundance. But remember, whether or not these people were born into wealth, most of them worked very hard for long periods of time, doing work they sometimes did not enjoy doing. But they chased a dream... and caught it. Even Brad Pitt dressed up like a chicken while advertising a chicken restaurant, and he sold cigarettes, among many other odd jobs he held.

One common factor of successful people is they have a dream and they pursue it. Life may not always be easy, but it can be full and rewarding.

And yes, there are successful people who have misplaced priorities, who placed the pursuit of money first and in doing this, lost their loved ones, their health, and their real friends. I do not think of them as wealthy or abundant. I think of those folks as being impoverished and, in the end, empty and alone.

So, to "act as though" when placing your intention on financial abundance is to walk the walk of the responsible wealthy. Decide what you would really enjoy doing in life. You may really enjoy fixing cars, driving cars, building homes, making cookies, cooking entrees, working with numbers, working with hair and beauty products, talking to people, helping people, saving animals, etc. You need to know what you love in order to create the dream you decide to chase. Place your intention on the end result of that dream. If you know you would love to own a real estate agency, begin by getting a real estate sales license. If you know you would love to rescue people, begin to take first responder classes. A chapter is dedicated to Goals and Deliberate Creation and speaks to these issues.

The same thing applies to losing weight or getting physically fit. If you decide to set your intention on being physically fit or losing 20 or 100 pounds, you have to "act as though" you are physically fit and are already at your perfect weight/fat/muscle ratio. Does that mean you buy a bikini and look at it as a reminder of your intention, hoping that your body will simply respond to your intention? Fit people do not do that. Fit people exercise regularly and eat healthily. People who are at their perfect weight don't get there by grazing from the couch every night eating chips while watching TV. (I can say this from experience.)

Fit people don't spend the day thinking about food or snacks. A fit person enjoys food and will eat what he or she wants to eat – but it is rare that you will see a person who is already physically fit munching on junk and drinking to excess. Yes, I know athletes can eat and drink like this during the time they are involved with daily exercise and high physical activity. But once the athlete retires from, let's say football, if the poor eating and drinking behavior continues – he will quickly gain weight as the muscle is replaced with fat.

So, to "act as though" means to act as the fit person acts. This may mean you begin by going for a five-minute walk every day and reducing your calorie intake by 100 calories a day for a period of time. And when you finally go from fat to fit, you will be walking or running each day (or going to a fitness center, playing softball, or some form of physical fitness enjoyment) and you will continue to be "acting as though" until you become the end result you seek.

Just do not get to your goal and become like the retired athlete who, instead of maintaining his or her fitness, begins to graze and drink because his or her body – at this time – is fit. Do not let yourself become unfit.

What does all this mean??

It all goes back to being citizens of two worlds. We live in both the physical world with limitation and in the quantum world of deliberate creation.

The BIG difference for us is this: we recognize our limitations, but we also recognize our spiritual heritage. We can set an intention with confidence, knowing that opportunities will come to us for us to act upon and become financially abundant, physically fit, spiritually enlightened, and so on. We do not have to accept failure, nor are we alone on our journey. We are aware of the Universe (God) that will deliver opportunities to you that you will then act upon to make your dream manifest.

Act "As Though"

Native American Code of Ethics

A friend shared this with me years ago and I'd like to share it with you now.

Native American Code of Ethics

1. Rise with the sun to pray. Pray alone. Pray often. The Great Spirit will listen, if you only speak.

2. Be tolerant of those who are lost on their path. Ignorance, conceit, anger, jealousy, and greed stem from a lost soul. Pray that they will find guidance.

3. Search for yourself, by yourself. Do not allow others to make your path for you. It is your road and yours alone. Others may walk it with you, but no one can walk it for you.

4. Treat the guests in your home with much consideration. Serve them the best food, give them the best bed and treat them with respect and honor.

5. Do not take what is not yours, whether from a person, a community, the wilderness, or from a culture. It was not earned nor given. It is not yours.

6. Respect all things that are placed upon this earth – whether people or plant.

7. Honor other people's thoughts, wishes, and words. Never interrupt another or mock or rudely mimic them. Allow each person the right to personal expression.

8. Never speak of others in a bad way. The negative energy that you put out into the Universe will multiply when it returns to you.

9. All persons make mistakes. And all mistakes can be forgiven.

10. Bad thoughts cause illness of the mind, body, and spirit. Practice optimism.

11. Nature is not FOR us, it is a PART of us. They are part of your worldly family.

12. Children are the seeds of our future. Plant love in their hearts and water them with wisdom and life's lessons. When they are grown, give them space to grow.

13. Avoid hurting the hearts of others. The poison of your pain will return to you.

14. Be truthful at all times. Honesty is the test of one's will within this Universe.

15. Keep yourself balanced. Your mental self, spiritual self, emotional self, and physical self all need to be strong, pure, and healthy. Work out the body to strengthen the mind. Grow rich in spirit to cure emotional ails.

16. Make conscious decisions as to who you will be and how you will react. Be responsible for your own actions.

17. Respect the privacy and personal space of others. Do not touch the personal property of others, especially sacred and religious objects. This is forbidden.

18. Be true to yourself first. You cannot nurture and help others if you cannot nurture and help yourself first.

19. Respect others' religious beliefs. Do not force your belief on others.

20. Share your good fortune with others. Participate in charity.

Author unknown

Chapter 9
Manifesting Exercises

T he magic box mentioned in the book *Not Manifesting? This Book is for You!* is a vehicle I use to successfully "let go" of my intention. It seems that one of the most difficult challenges we face in manifesting our desires is to let go of our intention and, at the same time, to remain focused on our intention. It seems contradictory, but it's really not contradictory at all.

When you hope you get a new vehicle, you tend to daydream about it and notice nice cars and wish you had one of them. You might notice the new Honda CRV, see yourself driving it and wish you had one. You might think that having a new black Honda

CRV with a roof rack, running boards, and a sun-roof would be great. Then you may notice the newly designed Toyota Rav4 and think to yourself what a nice-looking vehicle the Rav4 has become, and begin to daydream about the Rav4.

However, when you intend to buy a new vehicle, you will study the models that interest you. Your study goes well beyond a sunroof and running boards. If you are like most of us, when you intend to buy a new vehicle, you will research several models about their safety, reliability, gas mileage, comfort, affordability, and so on. You will visit manufacturers' websites to compare packages. You will visit a website like the Kelly Blue Book to check trade-in values. You may go to *Consumer Reports* to research reliability. When you *intend* to purchase a vehicle, you are constantly refining your search. When you have narrowed your search down to two or three vehicles, it is then you will test drive. Some people actually rent the vehicle for a weekend or a week instead of test driving at the dealership so they can test drive it for days instead of taking it for a 30-minute spin with the salesperson sitting in the jump seat.

- When we intend to accomplish something, we are riveted on it.
- When we are wishing or hoping, we pretty much ride on the surface.

Manifesting Exercises

- When we intend to accomplish something, we consistently move toward our objective without any doubt that we will eventually arrive.
- When we are wishing and hoping, we tend to be all over the place and distracted by new thoughts bombarding our minds.

When you intend to accomplish something, you are riveted but you remain open to the idea that there may be something better for you as you do the research. You may eventually decide to purchase a four-door sedan rather than the crossover because, along the way, it became clear to you the four-door sedan would better serve you.

Now, as you walk along this path of intending to purchase a new vehicle, perhaps it becomes clear to you that, for some reason, it is not a good time for you to do it. More importantly, it's not a big deal to you. You might feel a little disappointed, but you are nonetheless in fine shape despite the wear and tear of your research. You continue to drive the vehicle you currently own until you are in a position to purchase a new one. And you don't lose any sleep over it.

Boil this example down to the message and you get the following:

Wishing and hoping is not remotely related to deliberate creation.

Intention includes action and constantly moving toward.
The outcome is not the hill you will die on, so you can easily let go.

When you decide to place an intention, make sure it is not emotionally charged. If the outcome of your intention will mean the ability to meet your basic life needs, then it is emotionally charged. If the outcome of your intention is to avoid eviction at the end of the month – well, that is certainly emotionally charged. There is no way that you could place that intention into the magic box and let it go. You would be worried every minute of the day and tossing and turning at night, as you thought about the impending eviction.

The intention you place to the Universe for your first deliberate creation must be one you can walk away from and live without. You ask yourself how you would feel if you did not attract that particular intention. If you can honestly say you'd be OK with it, then that is the intention with which to work. But also, make your intention big enough to make a difference in your life and believable enough to your ego that your ego will give it a pass-through. The type of intention I recommend is attracting a person or event into your life or manifesting a higher-paying position in the workplace.

Next, I'd like to introduce you to an exercise that I

have shared with several readers who emailed me telling me they were not having any success manifesting.

If you have been involved with the Law of Attraction for long and you have not been able to create, you may be struggling with belief issues. Beliefs are VERY STRONG.

Someone who is afraid of heights will experience physical responses when standing on a high place, such as a roof, or even looking out the window of a tall hotel. Typically, their legs will get weak, their knees will weaken, and they may feel light-headed and begin to panic, even though they are in no danger at all. Considering that their irrational fear of heights even causes physical reactions, we can understand that when we really believe something to be true, it is really difficult to change that belief. Affirmations and positive thinking may not be deep enough to cause a real change or a shift in a belief. The person who fears heights can say to him or herself over and over that the fear is baseless – but that knowledge will not convince his or her belief and that person will continue to have weak legs until they move away from the window or come down from the roof.

Somewhere along the way, you may have picked up the belief that you are not worthy of succeeding in the areas where you seem stuck (or something similar). You may not even remember what caused this belief to happen. Our first beliefs came to us when we were infants, when we learn from our parents and the people who surround us and communicate with us or within our earshot. This can happen, for instance, when we hear or feel our parents worrying about money, paying bills, and so on.

Now, on to the exercise!

Exercise with Orange Juice

Having said that, I'd like you to try an exercise that has absolutely nothing to do with belief but has everything to do with the power you have – the power that you are. This will give you change immediately.

When you realize that you can actually change the molecular make-up of matter, you can go on to make many changes in other areas.

I recommend you perform this exercise using orange juice because orange juice has a strong taste. You can use any liquid you want, but make sure it has a strong taste that causes your tongue to stand up and take notice when you drink it. For this reason, I will be referring to orange juice in the following exercise.

Manifesting Exercises

Take two glasses and pour orange juice into each of them. Take one glass and set it on a table where you can sit comfortably and also where you can see a timer. I suggest using the kitchen table because, from there, you can usually see the oven or micro-wave timer.

Then place the other glass of orange juice in a different room from where you are.

Set your oven timer for two minutes, return to the glass of orange juice on your kitchen table, sit down, and clear your thoughts.

When the first minute elapses and the final minute begins, both think and say out loud to the juice that you love and appreciate it. Focus your feelings and become riveted on your glass of orange juice. Think of its taste on your tongue – breathe in its fragrance – keep thinking and feeling and saying to the juice that you love and appreciate it – that you are grateful for it –that you appreciate and love it. Focus on the glass of orange juice, hold it in your hands, sent it your love and appreciation. Talk out loud. FEEL the love. FEEL the appreciation. When the timer bell goes off, the work is over. Stop.

Now taste your drink. After tasting the orange juice you spent one minute of time fully focused on, go taste the other glass of juice you left in the other room. You will notice they taste different. The one you sent love and gratitude to for that minute tastes smoother and maybe sweeter (depending what drink you are using).

You have proven to yourself (your ego) that your focus, your riveted message in feelings of love, gratitude, and appreciation actually changed the molecular structure of the orange juice. You have just deliberately created a different drink from the one you had poured minutes earlier. You have proven that deliberate creation is genuine. The ego will now have no choice but to believe in your power.

After you master that, do the same thing with an intention. Picture a person or event as your intention, then use your imagination to place your intention in your cupped hands. Using the same method as when you changed the taste of the orange juice, send to the pictured person or event your love and appreciation – and FEEL it. Do this for ONE minute and only for one minute. You need to concentrate your power and you need to feel strongly.

If your intention is to forgive someone in your life (in order to remove blockages to the flowing of your energy), you will see that, by doing this a few times each day, your unforgiveness will fall away. *It is the act of sending genuine love and appreciation in a focused stream of energy that makes all the difference.* You can do this to attract a person (you don't have to know the person now) or an event. Please do not use this concentrated energy to attract things such as parking spaces. Instead use this exercise to attract something into your life that will change your life for the better. The event could even be an additional stream of income, but *do not let this be an emotionally charged manifestation.*

Do this exercise up to four times a day, but NEVER do it for more than one minute. After a minute, we begin to think instead of feel. This highly concentrated focus/feeling actually changes the molecules of the juice! As you know, the Law of Attraction teaches that we attract into our lives whatever we focus on and that like attracts like. Quantum physics teaches us that there are no limitations because everything is made of vibrating energy. You will be sending out a very powerful intention to the Universe, and quantum physics is the tool that will work on your behalf. However, the missing piece for many people is the focused love, gratitude, and appreciation. That missing piece will cause miracles to occur in your life!

It may take a few weeks or longer to see the desired intention coming to you. The Universe will send opportunities or ideas for opportunities. Act on those ideas or opportunities and do not give up.

The focus in this exercise is actually reaching into your heart and sending love, appreciation, gratitude, and forgiveness. It is the power of love and appreciation that moves molecules. The power you seek is within you!

The more success you have with each deliberate creation, the quicker the Universe will deliver your results. As you move ahead with deliberate creation, you will come to a time in your life when you will know what you should be creating on a daily basis in order to live your life on purpose, and with purpose, each day.

Do not make the mistake of thinking that the Universe is Santa in disguise. We have come here to this life with tools to create, lessons to learn, and love to discover.

Chapter 10
Engaging Your Many Resources

This exercise works for me when I want to attract a person or event into my life. It has worked to attract people, job promotions, and creative ideas that I apply to my work and my life.

This is the time I call upon the Universe, my angels, spirit guides, and loved ones who have passed. I never leave anyone out and I believe that those who come to me are the right helpers to work on my request. It's much like the magic box. With the box, I call on everyone and let them know what I intend to co-create. For this exercise of walking and talking, I call on everyone every day.

Living the Law of Attraction

If you are able to take a walk first thing in the morning, make sure it's early because you will be talking out loud and people may think you are talking to yourself. Go for your walk when you feel comfortable talking out loud and when you feel it's safe to talk.

I begin my walk talking to God, my angels, my spirit guides, and my loved ones. Sometimes I talk to them as if we were all walking in a big group, and sometimes I talk to them one at a time.

I tell them clearly what I need them to do on my behalf. I realize they are not deaf and they heard me the first time, but I have this conversation with them every day – and every day I thank them for working on my behalf.

You may think at this point that I am advising you to not detach from the outcome. Nothing of the sort. Having this conversation every day keeps your attention riveted. But, because you are having a conversation with your angels, guides, loved ones, God, Jesus, etc., you are not worried about the outcome because you have placed your intention in the hands and hearts of those who love you.

My walk is only 30 minutes, but it's the best 30 minutes of the day.

When I began doing this exercise several years ago,

Engaging Your Many Resources

I felt like I was talking to myself. I felt quite fool-ish, but I decided to trust in the process and trust in the God, angels, spirit guides, and in the love of the people in my life who had passed. Well, trusting paid off!

If you desire to attract a meaningful relationship into your life, first take the time to figure out what is important to you in a person.

A shallow person may demand that the person they attract be either "a hunk" or be "hot." People are so much more than their bodies and their looks. Have you ever met a really attractive person, but then found them less attractive as you got to know them? Or have you ever met a plain-looking person who became more attractive as you got to know them? The real attraction begins when you are seeing with your heart.

There is a story written for children, but best read by adults, called *The Little Prince* by Antoine de Saint-Exupéry. One of the lessons in this story tells us, "It is only with the heart that one can see rightly. What is essential is invisible to the eye." This is the wisdom I am speaking of when I ask you what you consider important values and traits in a person.

If your only desire is to meet somebody with a great body, then you are missing the point of this book and you are surfing on the surface of life. But if you want to be able to love and be loved, then pay close attention to this exercise.

Many years ago, I subscribed to the idea that "all the good ones are taken." I decided to try this walking and talking exercise to attract a person into my life. I decided the person who matched my most important areas of interest would be a man who was financially independent, six feet tall (how trite), kind, an animal lover, and someone who respected me.

Sound like a tall order? I met a few men who were very nice but we did not click (and they did not fit the request). Then, within 45 days, I met a man named Michael. He was everything I asked for – kind, animal lover, etc. We dated for a year. We decided not to marry, but after all these years we remain very close. Michael was in many ways the perfect companion for me, but I learned that in many other ways, he was not.

I am a die-hard Pats fan. (In case you don't know this, they are the New England Patriots, Boston's football team.) I loved the Pats when they couldn't win a game even if the other team didn't show up for the game! I'd watch them when they were "playing for pride" – whatever that means. Now they have won some Super Bowls, had Spygate, human growth hormones, drug arrests, and who knows what else is coming down the road! But I still love them. Spygate is and was embarrassing – you shouldn't have to cheat to win, regardless of all the pressure and the millions of dollars changing hands. Activities like Spygate are things I will never understand.

Yes, I love to watch football and I like doing things outside the house. Next weekend I am meeting friends at a place called Lake Francis for a few days. It's about 15 miles from the Canadian border. We plan to kayak, moose watch, go for walks or hikes, and cook by a campfire. My friends are already there on vacation and are camping at the lake. My companion and I will be staying in a rented cabin for the weekend. The reason for this is that, although I enjoy adventure, it must include comfortable beds, hot showers, microwaves … the comforts of home. (Sad, huh?)

I am sharing this because I want you to know that when I was doing the walking and talking exercise, I forgot to mention a few very important aspects of what I wanted to my angels, guides, and loved ones when I was placing my order.

The fact that Michael was six feet tall and financially sound in the end did not matter in sustaining the relationship. What did matter was that he loved animals, was kind, and was a gentleman in every sense of the word.

But in all this, I forgot to consider that I really do love football. I really do enjoy every minute of it. When the summer is winding down, I look forward to football season so I do not mourn the passing of summer.

I appreciate just about any sport and any gymnastic event. I may never ski off ski jumps – in fact, I may never ski at all. But I appreciate the folks who do and I love to watch them. I like to play golf but I can't seem to get myself to watch it on TV. It's boring.

I'm not a great golfer and I wish the course were 14 holes instead of 18 holes. It seems that I'm good for 14 holes and then I'm just looking forward to the 19th hole where I can enjoy a hamburger and a drink. If I play two above par per hole, I am psyched. If I 10-out on a par 3, I just move on to the next hole and look forward to the 19th hole. In other words, it doesn't matter if I'm doing well or not. I just enjoy the game.

I also forgot to consider that I really do enjoy creative activities like cooking, painting, drawing, and writing.

Michael did not fit the bill on those items. He had absolutely no interest in sports at all. He did not have a creative bone in his body. Michael's idea of a good time was to sit at home watching movies or reading a book. Yes, I got what I asked for, but I ended up bored out of my skull on most weekends as I was trying to make things work.

So if I were to take that particular walk all over again, knowing what I know now, I'd describe a man who loves animals, is kind, is a gentleman, appreciates sports, who likes adventure, and enjoys sharing creative activities. I'd also want to attract someone who is independent as well as interdependent (in other words, not needy).

Also, when taking the deliberate creation walk, be aware of nature around you. Breathe in the air. Notice birds, flowers, trees, sky, and clouds. Appreciate the gift of life God has created for our playground – take it all in and be one with it. I know that when I include love and appreciation for all that I encounter, my intentions manifest more quickly.

Most important, then, when you want to attract a person into your life with the intention of creating a meaningful relationship, is seeking to attract the values you possess in yourself and the values you respect in others. Focus on values.

Chapter 11
Plugging Into Source Energy

This part is for you, whether you are new to the kingdom within and plugging into Source Energy or you just need a place in which to start recognizing your power. You need to acknowledge that there is a higher power inside you and you need to be open to this presence within. You have to recognize that the Universe or God is everywhere – inside of you and outside of you. You are an extension of God. You have the kingdom of God within, waiting to be recognized and released.

You may have heard the term "still small voice within." That still small voice is your center of power. But you need to be able to access that oh-sogentle power within. You will need to make a special time each day to spend in deliberate contact with your higher power. As you begin to make contact with your higher power and begin plugging into Source Energy, you will see your life begin to change. This unleashing of your power within is not a quick fix, nor is it a drive-up window experience. This is a daily, deliberate encounter that will strengthen your inner knowing and your confidence in your ability to reject the doubts created by your ego.

Begin by setting aside 15 minutes of time each day. Sit in a comfortable chair and relax. This is not a meditation so much as it is inner listening. Acknowledge the spirit of God within. Be quiet and begin to connect with your higher self by asking that your higher self be revealed to you. You may sit in quiet for quite a few minutes, but at some point you will feel some form of contact. When you feel this contact, place your intention that your higher self has revealed to you. Give yourself to your higher power – give yourself to the Universe (plug into Source) and ask to live in spiritual awareness and awakeness (live your walk from Source energy). Invite Source Energy (God, the Universe, or whatever title you use to address our creator) to operate to the fullest potential in your life and surrender yourself to God (or Source Energy, the Universe, etc). Vow to live each day by the leadership of Spirit instead of the smallness of ego desires.

Plugging Into Source Energy

When you have mastered the act of self surrender, continue to do this exercise 15 minutes each day. When you feel the connection, then ask the Universe (God) to bring you your desired intention. Be sincere and be humble. You will experience astonishing results as you practice this quiet communication. And, as you continue to practice this quiet communication, begin to focus on your heart chakra. Your heart chakra is the energy center in the middle of your chest and is associated with your heart. This is where feelings of love originate. This is where happiness, joy, compassion, and appreciation originate. You will begin to understand that the spirit of God within you is larger and closer than your heart, your mind, or your body. You will be amazed when you realize the power within you and that this power is easily accessed through your focused love, forgiveness, appreciation, and gratitude.

As you continue to communicate with the Universe using this quiet, reverent technique, you will begin to naturally frame your intentions to attract love, kindness, spiritual insight, etc., as your walk in spirit becomes larger than your walk in the ego. You may have begun the Law of Attraction journey wanting to feed your ego by manifesting flashy cars or Malibu homes, but you will notice the ego desires fall away as your spiritual self begins to thirst for higher vibrational rewards. Yes, *of course* you can have the car and the home – but you can also have the spiritual rewards that make your life path exciting and fulfilling. Your life will become a life of serendipity.

When you learn to engage the Universe through recognizing the kingdom of God within and plugging into Source Energy, you will also learn to trust the Universe. The act of letting go of the outcome is really the depth of your trust in the Universe in the act of self-surrender. Trusting the Universe is much larger and deeper than you might suspect. The tiny ego we rely on tries its very best to throw doubt in our path so we do not fully engage and plug into the Universe but instead fearfully hold on to the tiniest bit of self-defeating doubt.

The tightrope walk begins when we start to fully and completely trust the Universe by our baby steps of deliberate creation. The more success we have, the more we trust. However, I DO NOT recommend that you simply throw caution to the wind and jump off the trust cliff! This is a spiritual growth process and it takes many steps of success for us to grow into a natural place of trust.

So in the beginning of your manifesting exercises, you will notice that the more you succeed … well, the more you succeed! It's just like when you learned to ride a bicycle or drive a car. At first you may have been unsure and possibly fearful – but you were also excited and full of expectation. You had your share of bike falls and car dents and then, one day, you noticed you could ride your bike or drive your car just as if it were an extension of yourself. It took time for you to learn these lessons and it will take time to learn to live a serendipitous life.

Lastly, I'd like to refer you to a channeled book written in 1988 by Sanaya Roman and Duane Packer. The title of this book is *Creating Money*. The ISBN is 0-915811-09X. The good news is that this book is no longer a hard-to-find older book because it is on Amazon, having been reprinted.

Creating Money is a turning point book that I happened to pick up twenty years ago. I remember flipping through the table of contents and quickly realizing that the book I held in my hands was based on spiritual experimentation and not some kind of get-rich-quick scheme.

Creating Money gives several manifesting exercises that really did work for me. The exercises can seem quite involved and complicated because they involve steps. But if you take the time to read them thoroughly and let them sink into your mind, you will absorb what you need in order to do the exercises. These exercises are actually done with your heart and they do not require you to memorize. I found those early exercises good practice. I do know that not all authors speak to all people because each of us has a different learning style.

However, I did benefit from some very profound words; some I mention below.

Even twenty years ago, these authors were reminding us that abundance is our natural state and that money will flow in your life when you are doing what you love.

I remember reading the following words, found (in the original book) on page 168. "Don't let other people's pictures of what you ought to be doing determine what you do," and, "It is best to follow your own wisdom. If things turn out well, you will know you did it yourself, and have more trust and confidence in yourself…"

If you are not familiar with this book, I recommend you buy it or pick it up at your library. I still have my original copy, 20 years later.

Chapter 12
Manifesting Stories

W hen I talk about living a serendipitous life, I mean that you can live a life where everything seems to just fall into place. When difficult challenges confront you, you expect an outcome that leaves you in a better condition than you were before the challenge. When you set your intention to deliberately manifest your heart's desires, you naturally expect the Universe to deliver whatever your intention is, or better. You may desire to attract a new car or a new house. Perhaps your intention is to attract greater success in your business or career. Maybe your point of focus is to attract the perfect partner for you to spend the rest of your life learning to love. For the vast majority of us, these are the big-ticket manifesting items.

By seeking and surrendering and plugging into the kingdom of God within, you are living each day at a higher vibration and your life becomes serendipitous. Your days become easier for you because daily events work to your advantage. You don't need to set your intention to find a parking space. Instead, you expect to see parking spaces when and where you need them. If you'd prefer to get the exercise and walk a reasonable distance from your parking space to your destination, you will find one there for you. If you are in a hurry and need to find a space near your destination, it will be there waiting for you. It becomes a genuine surprise if a convenient parking space is not made available to you. You come to expect the best in everyday things. If an unfortunate event happens in your day, you expect a positive outcome because you know a positive outcome will happen.

This serendipitous life of which I speak is lived in the daily ordinary life. I am not talking about the big-ticket intentions I mentioned in the first paragraph, nor am I talking about being let go from a job or other big, emotionally charged events. I am talking about what some people would call "small stuff." However, if you live a serendipitous life, the repeated small stuff becomes huge for you.

For example, one day at work at about midmorning, I received an email saying that someone had noticed that my vehicle had a flat tire. They believed it was my vehicle because it had a "Life is Good" wheel cover on the back of it.

I gathered my things (wallet with my AAA membership card, etc.) and walked to the elevator. It took seconds for the elevator to stop at my floor. As the elevator descended to the ground level, my response was said out loud (I was alone in the elevator): "for my best and highest good."

When I got to the front door of the building, it was raining and kind of raw outside, but my car was in a parking garage. That in itself lessened the potential negative impact on me and on the AAA man I thought I might be calling to change the tire. My hope was that the tire had enough air in it so I could drive to a gas station and fill it with air or drive it to a tire place and have it fixed if it had picked up a nail or the like.

I got out to the garage and saw that my vehicle was tilted. Yes, the tire was flat – really, really flat. Thankfully, the parking space next to my vehicle on the side of the flat tire was empty, which was very unusual because those spaces are premium spaces. I had the original spare tire on the back of my CRV so I knew the tire swap would be successful.

I then called AAA for assistance. My intention was

to have my tire changed, have the original one fixed and then have them changed back to the original set. My four tires were old and I planned to discard them in a couple of months when I bought four snow tires. My CRV has all-wheel drive and it does drive well in the winter with all-season radials on it – but it drives fantastically with four snow tires instead. If you have to use snow tires in the winter, consider putting them all around instead of buying just two of them. I had a Toyota Celica before the Honda CRV and did the same with my Celica. The Celica had front-wheel drive and using four snow tires made a big difference. I loved my Celica but at 250,000 miles, my mechanic told me to get rid of it because it had become a casket on wheels. That is why I now have the CRV. I see I am digressing!

So, back to my flat tire story.

I called AAA and as I was talking to them, a man named Mark appeared. He had entered the garage seconds behind me. Mark told me I could cancel my conversation with AAA because he would change the tire for me. I told AAA my knight had arrived.

Mark worked for Facilities in my department and, I found out later, Facilities had rules prohibiting the guys from doing things for the employees like changing tires. I imagine this had to do with insurance.

Anyway, Mark jacked the car up just enough to try using the tire iron to get the lug nuts off. Well, with all his strength, the lug nuts would not even budge an inch. He told me he'd be right back and disappeared into the building, then returned with a can of WD–40. He soaked the lug nuts with the substance and, about ten minutes later, he was able to get them off the wheel. I told him I would be bringing my tire to the Tire Warehouse for repair. He quickly inspected the tire and then he crouched to the ground to eyeball the other three tires.

Mark told me in no uncertain terms that all the tires were shot and needed to be replaced. He then put the spare on my car and placed the jack back into the jack space, put the wheel cover in the car, and fastened the flat tire where the spare had been. He told me there was absolutely no way the tire could be repaired. Mark showed me that I had driven the car for so many miles that the steel belts were coming out! He said I was very fortunate it did not blow out on the highway, where something far worse could have happened. I drive 60 miles round trip to work every day, using the highway.

As I was driving to Tire Warehouse, I was thinking that perhaps I could buy a used tire and continue to use these tires for a couple of months. I just did not want to spend $400 or more for a set of new tires at that time.

Living the Law of Attraction

When I arrived at Tire Warehouse, my parking space was waiting for me. There are four parking spaces they use to work on the cars. Usually, unless you get there first thing in the morning, there is a delay in service while you hang around waiting for a space to become available. But because I expect parking spaces to be there when I need them, I just smiled and thanked the Universe for reserving this space for me. I also knew that if the space was not available and a long wait was in store (over 30 minutes), I would know the Universe was actually indicating that I go up the road and check out Sam's Club instead. But with the open parking space welcoming me, I knew I was in the correct place.

The service man looked at my flat tire and gave me "the look" - you know, the look someone gives you when they are thinking you have got to have rocks in your head. He walked around the vehicle and checked the other three tires.

He said he had bad news. He told me it was a miracle I was standing there at all. The four tires were bald and two of the bald tires were beginning to lose the steel belts. He was kind enough to show me. He also said the tires were so dangerous that he could not allow me to drive away on them. After actually taking the time to look at the tires, I assure you that there is no way I would have driven another block on them.

I was prepared to buy the new tires so I was not attached to any particular outcome. He looked at the tire measurements and told me that this must be my lucky day. About 45 minutes before I arrived, a man had driven in with his new car and wanted his tires replaced with wider, flashier ones. So there were four brand-new Michelin tires that retailed for $150.00 each. The man at Tire Warehouse gave them to me for $20.00 each. My $600.00 Michelins cost me $80.00, plus mounting and balancing. Needless to say, I was very happy with the end result of a not-so-nice beginning.

Here's another example of serendipity on a much smaller scale.

I have a Border collie named Sam. Sammie is twelve years old but he thinks he is about three, at most. He spends his day playing and sleeping. If I am throwing the tennis ball for him and, at the same time, company drops by, Sam has no idea there is anyone or anything else in the yard other than the tennis ball and me. If you came to visit and brought a tennis ball, Sam would acknowledge only you and the tennis ball. I have had Border collies all my life. I only recommend you buy or adopt one if you have a big yard for interactive play and plenty of time to exercise him or her every day. They tend to be hyperactive for the first five years of life and then, between five and six years old, they become normal. They are very high energy and high activity. To top it off, Border collies are very intelligent.

Anyway, I had been meaning to buy a particular Border collie calendar this year, but had not thought of it when I was out shopping for Christmas presents. Finally, shortly after Christmas I went to the mall to get my calendar, but, not surprisingly, the calendars were pretty much sold out. I went to several stores in addition to the calendar kiosk. I could not find the calendar I wanted so I returned home empty-handed.

I was thinking about searching for a calendar while I was driving to work the next day. I figured that in the upcoming weeks I could find plenty of stores to go hunting for my calendar. I also considered ordering one online.

When I arrived at work one of the staff, named Paula, called me over to her desk. She handed me a wrapped Christmas gift. It was square and flat. I opened it to find... what else? A Border collie calendar! And it was the exact one I was hoping to find. I thanked Paula profusely and told her that she had made not only my day, but at least my week. I then went joyfully to the cafeteria and bought us blueberry muffins. Now, how wonderful was that?

Those are two examples of a serendipitous life. It is a life that just works for you. My life works for me and I want your life to work for you.

Chapter 13
Practical Hypnosis

We humans are creatures of habit. Most of us resist change. Even when we aren't getting the results that we desire, we cling to the comfort of the familiar. So we tend to live our lives thinking the same old thoughts, seeking (unconsciously, most of the time) experiences that reinforce our old familiar attitudes and behaviors. All of this can't help but produce the same old results.

Once you have decided that you need to change some of these things, one of the easiest ways to help it to happen in a safe and comfortable way is to use hypnosis.

Living the Law of Attraction

Unfortunately, many hypnosis websites claim that the Law of Attraction is the Universe's way to provide money and material goods automatically, and that you can use hypnosis to accelerate the process. If you have tried manifesting for purely materialistic purposes without success, it is unlikely that hypnosis will help. However, hypnosis *is* a valuable tool to help you apply the Law of Attraction as a way to live a serendipitous life.

Why? Let's look more closely at what hypnosis is. To do that, we need to look at the mind. Like an iceberg, 90 percent of our mind is below the surface of our everyday awareness. This part, the subconscious mind, keeps us alive by regulating bodily functions like heart rate, blood pressure, and respiration. It is also the storehouse of all our memories, feelings, and attitudes.

Hypnosis is a technique that gets the mind to focus on something: the voice of the hypnotist, a light or a spot on the wall. The act of focusing induces an altered state of consciousness, which is between waking and sleeping. While in this altered state, we have access to many of our subconscious thoughts and feelings, which are normally hidden from us. We are also more open to suggestion, and more amenable to accept positive changes. Hypnosis can help us change the way we think and the way we behave, and that, in turn, can change what we attract into our lives.

Practical Hypnosis

Hypnosis can help you break down internal barriers. It can help you overcome old programming. It can help you work through grief, or find forgiveness for yourself or for someone who has wronged you. Because you are a "spiritual being having a human experience," you can use transpersonal hypnosis to access your Higher Mind. You can explore past lives and their karmic effects on your life today. More importantly, by accessing your memories of the life-between-lives state, you can learn more about *why* you chose to incarnate here and now. What is your soul's purpose? What lessons did you come here to learn?

Hypnosis can help to bring about more rapid change in your attitudes and limiting beliefs. You can use hypnosis to get in touch with subconscious parts of your personality: your Inner Critic, for example, or your Inner Child. Hypnosis can help you loosen the bonds of unhealthy relationships without bitterness or recrimination.

Some of these issues can be approached via self-hypnosis but, for most people, it helps greatly to work with a skilled hypnotherapist. A good source for referrals to hypnotists who approach their discipline holistically is the National Association of Transpersonal Hypnotherapists (NATH). The NATH website is: *www.holistictree.com*. Click on the "Practitioner Database" link or go directly to *www.holistictree.com/noah*.

Chapter 14
Energy Healing and Psychics

I am including information on psychics and energy healers because when we are learning to manifest our heart's desires, we invariably hit stumbling blocks. Earlier, I spoke about hypnosis and the major impact it can have on removing blocks to your energy flow by overcoming limiting beliefs and so on.

About one-third of the hundreds of emails I received after my first book came out asked about psychic readings and energy healing. Because there was such an interest, I thought it would be a good idea to include some information and referrals in this second book.

Living the Law of Attraction

When we think about using the Bible as ammunition to pass judgments on people, we usually think of things like so-called Holy Wars and the Inquisition. Lately, the Bible debate entered into the 2004 election, when the country was made to fear that homosexual marriage would certainly dismantle traditional marriage. I'm not sure how that would happen, but I am sure it played big in that presidential election. Psychics are another group of people the Bible appears to condemn.

Even without the Bible, psychics get a bad reputation. You see them at fairs, willing to tell your future for $5.00. If you go to the beach, you will certainly see signs for psychic readings, no appointment necessary. If you'd like an email reading or a telephone reading, you can go straight to E-Bay and bid on any one of hundreds of psychics. You could also Google-search for psychics and turn up pages and pages of hits. For many people, psychics are a joke of sorts. For fundamentalist Christians and most other Christians, psychic powers are rooted in Satan and hell. Psychics can't seem to win in many arenas.

But, with all the hoopla, there must be something to all of this... right?

I looked up the dictionary definitions of *prophet* and *psychic*. Below are a couple of the many definitions I found. All the definitions were similar.

Energy Healing and Psychics

Prophet
1. An authoritative person who divines the future.
2. Someone who speaks by divine inspiration; someone who is an interpreter of the will of God.

Psychic
1. Outside of natural or scientific knowledge; spiritual.
2. Sensitive to influences or forces of a non-physical or supernatural nature.

The definitions are kind of close. It looks like the difference is between someone who is speaking from a gift from God and someone who is speaking from, I guess, a gift from God. I don't see much difference.

If we can take our judgmental attitude and leave it to the side, we should take a closer look at psychics. I believe that many of them are fakes, but I also believe that many psychics are genuine. You need to see the fruits of the tree. Are all psychics carnival acts? No, they are not. Are many of them carnival acts (whether they are employed by a carnival or not)? Yes, many are acting.

In fact, people can be stunned by a fake psychic who gives a "cold reading." A cold reading goes like this for a woman aged 20-30: "Your intuition shows that your instincts are usually right when it comes to your hunches about people. There is a relationship in your life that you take seriously. There is not a great deal of money in your life right now, but I see that changing in the not-too-distant future."

A cold reading for a male aged 20-30 will often go like this: "You appear to be in good health and you have quite a bit of strength. There are areas of your life where you can be lazy, but that is OK for now. But begin to consider using your energy more wisely and you could be living a very comfortable life in the not-so-distant future."

A reading for teenagers would include these basics: "You are a friendly person and you show very strong loyalty to select people. If you work hard, you will enjoy success. But I also see that you tend to be lazy and like to waste time by sleeping late on weekend mornings. However, you are very helpful in many ways but you sometimes wonder if your help is really noticed."

Cold readings are telling people in certain age groups general kinds of information that is usually found in those age groups anyway. If you are reading for an elderly person and notice a ring or the mark where a ring used to be, you might talk about seeing a lifetime companion. You might mention financial concerns. If the "mark" is dressed to the nines, that person may not have financial concerns for him or herself, but the financial worries could be for a younger person in their lives.

Cold readings can be found just about everywhere – so you know by the "fruits" that these are either dishonest people or providers of amusement. For most fair- and beach-goers, the cold readings do no harm and provide entertainment.

Now, what about real psychics? Do they exist? Yes, they exist. Are they evil and getting their information from the devil? I certainly doubt it, in the vast majority of cases. I can't tell you if famous psychics are the genuine article because I don't personally know any of the famous psychics on television.

Sylvia Brown is a famous psychic. She appears on television, she writes books, she does readings on the phone and in her office. Her website tells us that a phone reading with Silvia is $850.00 and a phone reading with her son Chris is $500.00. If nothing else, she is very successful in this business.

John Edwards recommends energy work with Sandi Zak. Sandi's website says:

"While some people may experience results after one session, most people need multiple sessions to achieve the goals they desire. This is similar to working with a personal trainer, where you are taught techniques to reach your goals. Great results come from commitment."

Each of Sandi's Energy Touch sessions, in person or long-distance, is $150 and lasts about one hour. Is Sandi an effective energy worker? My guess is that she is very effective, just by the fact that John Edwards recommends her on his website.

One of the common themes I have noticed, however, is that for some of us, psychic reading and energy work can be quite expensive. I decided that it would be in the best interest of my readers if I referred them to effective practitioners I know and trust.

Chapter 15
Energy Healing

The person I recommend for energy work is the same person I recommended in my earlier book, *Not Manifesting? This Book is for You!* Her name is Marlene Campbell and her website is *http://www.rippleeffectworkshops.com/.*

I called Marlene to ask her if she would write a description about energy healing. I was surprised when I called the main phone number listed on her website and got an answering service that redirected me to another phone number. I called that number and Marlene answered on the first ring. She was on vacation at the Cape, walking along the beach with her husband. When I asked her why she would answer while she is on vacation, I was not surprised to hear her say that she wanted to be available if someone needed to connect with her.

I asked her if she would write about 1,000 words describing energy work and asked if she would discuss if this could be done remotely. I was especially interested in remote work so readers could benefit from energy work regardless of their location. She said she would be pleased to do it. The following description is written by Marlene. I hope you enjoy the information she shares.

"Remote Healing, also known as Long Distance Healing or Non-Local Healing, is healing that is done through principles of Quantum Physics. Physicists are aware that everything around us is made of energy. Our bodies are composed of electrical vibrations. Everything in the world is energy and electrical pulses in one form or another. The building blocks of matter are energy particles, or quanta, which are constantly freely moving.

Quantum physics principles state that everything is connected by energy; therefore, distance is not a factor. Everything is part of a continuous whole. Subatomic particles, or energy particles, change shape depending upon whether they are observed or not by other energy. By observing subatomic matter, therefore, we can influence subatomic matter. With an understanding of these principles comes an understanding of why remote healing is just as effective as healing sessions conducted in person.

Michael Talbot writes in *Holographic Universe*: 'In 1982 a remarkable event took place. At the University of Paris a research team led by physicist Alain Aspect performed what may turn out to be one of the most important experiments of the 20th century. Aspect and his team discovered that under certain circumstances subatomic particles such as electrons are able to instantaneously communicate with each other regardless of the distance separating them. It doesn't matter whether they are 10 feet or 10 billion miles apart.'

In addition Talbot writes this about David Bohm, a well-known physicist: 'This insight suggested to Bohm another way of understanding Aspect's discovery. Bohm believes the reason subatomic particles are able to remain in contact with one another regardless of the distance separating them is not because they are sending some sort of mysterious signal back and forth, but because their separateness is an illusion. He argues that at some deeper level of reality such particles are not individual entities, but are actually extensions of the same fundamental something.'

Scientists are now recognizing what mystics from many traditions have said for thousands of years – we are all connected and we are not separate. Dr

Norman Shealy, Founding President of the American Holistic Medical Association, had devised a test he has used for decades on famous people that he termed 'world-class healers.' He found that some of them actually had the ability to dramatically affect a subject's EEG readout from a distance when the subject did not know that they were receiving a distant healing. In addition, **many of Shealy's staff were trained in the modality Quantum-Touch®, and they, too, were able to demonstrate that even without touching the patient (!) they were capable of changing the electroencephalogram.**

In 1988 cardiologist Randolph Byrd conducted a rigidly designed, randomized, double-blind experiment to determine the effects of prayer, a form of remote healing, on patients in the Coronary Care Unit at San Francisco General Hospital over a ten-month period. A computer made the random assignments of which of the 383 newly-admitted patients involved in this study would be prayed for, and which would not. The statistically significant findings of this study were that prayed-for patients were five times less likely to require antibiotics, three times less likely to develop pulmonary edema... and none of the prayed-for patients required endotracheal intubation, whereas twelve of the non-prayed-for patients required this procedure.

In addition to these two studies mentioned, research studies have been conducted on energy healing at major universities and centers throughout the world. This information can be found in many books. *Vibrational Medicine* by Richard Gerber, *The Genie in Your Genes* by Dawson Church, *The Field* by Lynn McTaggart, *The Spontaneous Healing of Belief* by Gregg Braden, and *Power Versus Force* by David Hawkins are five sources.

The human body has an innate wisdom about how to heal itself. Deepak Chopra wrote, 'To promote the healing response, you must get past the grosser level of the body – cells, tissues, organs, and systems – and arrive at a junction between the mind and matter - the point where consciousness actually starts to have an effect.' But when your body does not have the energy that it needs to heal itself from an injury, illness, or a compromised immune system, Quantum-Touch® can provide a powerful field of energy that the body can entrain to.

A Quantum-Touch® energy healing session, whether in person or remotely, involves the principles of resonance and entrainment. When two things vibrate or resonate at different frequencies there is a tendency for the vibrations to come together. This is known as entrainment. Most often, the slower vibration matches the faster one. When remote healing is done, this energy frequency is sent through an interweaving energy field or matrix that connects everything. Energy has no limitations or boundaries, making remote healing an effective form of healing for physical, mental, and emotional issues.

In creating this field of energy it is important to note the power that is contained when we use the energy of the heart. In *The Spontaneous Healing of Belief*, Gregg Braden states, 'Studies by the Institute of Heartmath have shown that the electrical strength of the heart's signal, measured by an electrocardiogram (EKG), is up to 60 times as great as the signal from the human brain, measured by an electroencephalogram (EEG), while the heart's magnetic field is as much as 5000 times stronger than that of the brain. What is important here is that both fields can change the atoms.'

The heart is the largest generator and strongest generator of a magnetic field in the human body. Our psychic textbooks tell us that if we change the energy of the electromagnetic field that surrounds matter, then we can change the atoms of that matter. The human heart does both.

By tuning into the feelings in our hearts, with the feelings of love and gratitude, harmony and peace, as if our heart's desires are already manifested, an energy is transmitted in the matrix and an electrical magnetic blueprint is created that allows the quantum stuff of matter to form around those blueprints. This energy has an effect on people, animals, plants, situations, and the Earth. This energy brings about physical, mental, emotional and spiritual healing.

Energy Healing

This is what a practitioner of remote or local healing does. This is what all human beings are capable of, for it is love, the universal vibration, that allows this transfer of healing energies. *Your Love Has Impact* and *Your Love is Valuable* (two Quantum-Touch® bumper stickers) are two simple statements that explain healing, which is truly health, harmony, and balance within each of us and on the Earth and beyond."

Marlene E. Campbell

If you are interested in energy work, I invite you to explore Marlene's website and to contact her with any additional questions you have.

Good Luck
With great love
Betty Lipton

Chapter 16
Psychic Readings

T he person I recommend for psychic work is Betty Lipton of Portsmouth, New Hampshire. Betty does her work in person and on the telephone.

Betty

I'd like to introduce you to Betty Lipton. She has been a friend for twenty years and she is psychic. Her website is: *http://www.thezodiaczone.com/*

As a matter of history, I met Betty twenty years ago when I attended a party. When I arrived at the party,

Living the Law of Attraction

I found out it was a "psychic" party. Betty was in another room in the house, separate from the room we were in munching on chips and wings and drinking beer and wine. One at a time, someone would be called to get his or her psychic reading. When I was called, I remember walking into the room and seeing Betty sitting at a card table, tarot cards before her. I sat down. She introduced herself, took my hand and began telling me my future. She told me that I really like my work but I would be changing work positions several times during my career and that I would write books that would help others. I remember thinking that I loved my work and there was no way I would be changing work positions, plus I knew I would never write a book.

After that first introduction, Betty and I became friends. Because I didn't really know about the psychic arena outside of tourist attraction areas and television shows, I saw Betty as simply a really nice person, falling in and out of love just like everyone else. She just had a different way of making a living. It was nice to appreciate Betty as a friend and see her as a regular person. Back then, I did not know if she was gifted or not.

I used to work close to Betty's business so it was nice to be able to visit and have lunch every now and then. On one occasion, Betty shared some psychic insights. Within a short time, what she said came to pass. I began to think Betty did have some accurate insight.

Eventually, I told some work friends about Betty and her psychic work. One woman named Beth went to see Betty and brought pictures with her. Beth is an attorney and was actually out to prove Betty was a fraud because she did not believe that psychics were on the level. According to Beth, Betty fanned through the pictures, stopping at a few of them. After seeing all the pictures, Betty told Beth that Beth's mother (the lady in one of the pictures) was at the point of choosing between medication and food. She said someone needed to go to see Beth's mother and check her food supply. Betty also told Beth that the little boy in the picture (Beth's nephew) had a rare disorder of some kind that would affect his muscles as he grew older, but that it could be corrected with the right tests and treatment.

Beth decided to call her sister in New York and ask her to go check on their mother. Just as Betty had said, the mother had very little food to eat but was not telling her daughters because she did not "want to be a burden." The mother told them how hard it was to live on a fixed income and trying to buy food and medication and juggling the increasing costs of rent and other expenses. Needless to say, the daughters took some financial responsibility for their mother, including having her move in with one of them full-time.

Beth then told her sister what Betty had said about her son. Her son was six years old and appeared to be in perfect health, but after the experience with her mother, Beth's sister brought the boy to the doctor. Tests were run and Betty was proven right again. The boy received the right treatment and the disorder was corrected.

Through the years, Betty has told me some future happenings for myself and she has been at least 95% accurate in her predictions. And of course, you know that she was right about me and writing books – even though back then I thought that the chances of my writing a book were slim to none.

Betty takes her gift very seriously. She cares about the people who come to see her and acts as a kind of counselor as she delivers her psychic impressions. She has a tremendous sense of humor, she is kind, and she has a big heart.

I went to see her one day recently and asked if she could contact people who had passed. She said she could in many instances. I asked her if she could contact my mother. If you have read my first book you know that my mother passed away about twenty years ago from the human form of mad cow disease (Creutzfeldt-Jakob disease).

Betty immediately said she was getting an impression of a Mary or a Margaret. Betty had no way of knowing that my mother's name was Mary and her mother, my grandmother, was named Margaret. Betty said that Mary stepped forward and said to tell me that she was sorry she had put so much pressure on me to return to the Catholic Church because she learned after crossing over that "there are many roads to the mountain top." She also thanked both my brother and me for playing the music for her when she was dying. She told me the transition was peaceful and she is living in a wonderful place. She asked me not to worry about her and to tell my brother that she loves him.

Betty had never met my mother nor had I told her about my mother. My mother used to go to a monastery every week and say novenas for me so that I would return to the Church. She was convinced that with enough prayer, somehow, God would redirect me and have me return to church. Very lovingly, she badgered me almost every time she saw me, telling me I had to return to the Church or I would be going to hell and that she loved me too much to let me go to hell.

Mom was close to death when she was diagnosed with Creutzfeldt Jakob disease while she was at Massachusetts General Hospital. She returned home in an ambulance. My brother and I made the house ready, hired a 24/7 nurse for her, and cared for her as she died. During those last few days of her life, my brother played the piano for her and I played her

Irish records. She loved my brother's piano playing and she loved Irish music. They always made her smile.

The words that Betty said had to be genuine because there is no possible way that she could have known any of this information.

Betty works in Portsmouth, New Hampshire and is the longest-residing psychic in that town; she has been practicing there since 1985. I believe the reason for her success is that her intention is to help people. She considers everyone who comes to see her important. She will do her best to help everyone, from routine matters to the spiritual and everything in between.

People from all across the country, with many different issues, call on Betty. I believe this is because Betty believes in giving positive information but will also alert her clients when she sees problems and she will counsel them to help them address matters of concern.

Betty is a medium as well as being psychic (as you read from my experience when she made contact with my mother). She uses tarot cards, touch vibration, and because she is clairaudient, she successfully makes strong psychic connections over the telephone. She is also in demand for private parties and other social functions.

Psychic Readings

Betty is also a health intuitive. Several years ago, she began asking me about my sugar levels and telling me I should see a doctor and get my sugar checked. Although I knew Betty well and considered her my friend, I dismissed what she had to say. Maybe it's because it is so easy to dismiss what our family members, friends, and loved ones have to say if it makes no sense to us, or if it's something we don't want to hear. I believed I was healthy, so every time Betty asked about my sugar levels I'd tell her that I'd check it out, then dismiss the advice.

One day I got a cut on my finger. Not a big deal, except, it took a week to heal and the wound would reopen every time I swung my driver. Because this little cut was ruining my golf games, I made an appointment with my doctor.

My doctor suspected diabetes because the cut was not healing. My blood test came back and indeed, I did have diabetes. My first thought was that Betty was right ¬ did I ever feel like an idiot! My finger healed by following my doctor's instructions, and once again I could swing a club without bleeding on the grip.

Now I'll quote from one of the many newspaper interviews with her. The reporter asked Betty, "What do you say to skeptics?"

Betty: We need to realize that there is a lot more to

what we can see in front of us. There are different levels of consciousness and reality. I have the ability to tap into different areas where most people can't. It's very hard to turn a skeptic around unless they have their own experience. You can tell someone how good a chocolate sundae is, but unless they experience it, they will never know."

Explore Betty's website where you can find information, client reviews, and more.

Yes, Betty is the real deal.

Chapter 17
Mediumship and Clairvoyance

Afew years ago, as I was driving to the grocery store, I heard a radio advertisement describing a public event: the appearance of a psychic medium named Dr. Allen Fahey. I am the youngest child in my immediate family and my extended family, and most of my relatives, including both my parents, are deceased. The event was local and there were still tickets available. Yes, I was intrigued.

I told my friend Dawn about this event. She was intrigued as well. Both of us bought tickets online. Shortly afterwards, the remaining tickets were sold out. I don't know how many people attended that day, but the place was packed. If you are ever able to attend one of Dr. Fahey's events, I recommend that you arrive at least 45 minutes early if you want to get a decent seat.

Dr. Fahey is very clear, both on his website and at the event I attended, that it is possible that not every ticket holder will get a psychic or spirit reading. This is because, like John Edward, Dr. Fahey is drawn to certain areas of the audience by loved ones who have arrived in spirit in order to communicate with those of us who are left behind.

Neither Dawn nor I was called upon that day, so we were somewhat disappointed. However, by the time we walked out of the room where the event was held, both Dawn and I were absolutely convinced of Dr. Fahey's authenticity. I had recently witnessed psychic medium John Holland at a local event and, of course, I had seen John Edward on television. Dr. Fahey conducted his sessions much like John Holland and John Edward. The many people he acknowledged through "seeing" the spirits of those near them obviously recognized all the nicknames, places, and events that Dr. Fahey described as he conveyed the many messages from the spirits who are on the other side.

Mediums such as Dr. Fahey make themselves available to those who have crossed over to the other side, acting as a bridge between two worlds so that communication can take place. Dr. Fahey uses his gift to relay messages from spirit. He does not make any promises that he will connect with the loved one of your selection because he will work with the spirit who presents most strongly.

I decided to email a request to Dr. Fahey. I asked him to connect with my mother. If you have read my first book, you know how much my mother meant to me and that she still means a lot to me even now.

Dr. Fahey, however, connected with my father instead. I emailed him to let him know I was disappointed that my mother was not there, but that I would be contacting him again in the future to try again to connect with her. You may be thinking that I must think my dad is chopped liver. Not true. I loved him very much. When I was a little girl, I was daddy's little girl. I always felt his presence and thought he was probably staying near me through this life.

Dr. Fahey wrote back and said, "Yes! Your mother was present, but as you know, I keep with who is the dominant spirit until given notice otherwise. Thus keeping with the motto, 'You will always get what you need in a reading, not what you want.' If I had moved over to just your mom, then your dad's messages would not have come through and the messages hold significance and link to your future life."

Dr. Fahey was right in his response. The information my dad had to convey to me was very significant. But perhaps sometime my mom will come through!

Mediumship is a *process,* in which the medium, under proper conditions, gets messages from those who have crossed over to the other side. Dr. Fahey works before live audiences throughout New England and down the eastern coast, including Florida. He works extensively through his guides, as well as through his psychic ability.

You can contact Dr. Fahey by email or by telephone.

I invite you to explore his website: *http://www.hellofromheaven.com.*

floatation device was not going to be of much help to me in the event of a water landing. I pretty much felt that if God wanted me to fly, he would have given me wings.

In the mid-1990s, I decided to grit my teeth, have a drink, and fly to destinations more than 300 miles away. I still did not like flying, but it was practical and I am nothing if not practical. My family lives far enough away that in order to see them more than once a year, I needed to fly the friendly skies. Generally, my adventures in the sky seemed to be going along well, despite white knuckles and Makers Mark (a Kentucky bourbon).

But on the morning of September 11, 2001, my life and the lives of all Americans changed dramatically. I was at work, and staff came to my office to get me because the tragedy was being shown live on the television in the staff lounge. The first tower had been hit by the airliner and everyone was looking at the television screen in shock. Then I watched as the second plane hit the second tower and my heart sank to my feet as I realized we were under attack. There was no way that a second plane flying into the second tower was accidental. I was distraught and sickened for the people in the towers and the passengers on the planes. I felt broken in half. Watching our heroes in uniform run into the towers to save thousands of people, and then seeing the towers fall on our heroes and knowing many people were trapped inside, was just too much to take in. None of this was making any sense to me or to anyone around me. There were staff who had loved ones flying that day and a few of our staff had loved ones who worked near the towers. It was and still is a horrible time in our American days. Our whole nation experienced the anguish of the loss of thousands of lives in this evil act of capturing hundreds of passengers and creating suicide weapons out of commercial airliners. We could only imagine the horror and heartbreak of the innocent passengers and their distraught families. At the same time, we witnessed the many people who were desperately searching for loved ones by posting pictures and walking the streets. The suicide flight into the Pentagon brought chaos to Washington. Air force jets were flying just over the buildings in the effort to protect the Capitol and all the people who live and work in the Washington, D.C. area.

United Airlines Flight 93 was one of the hijacked planes. It did not reach Washington that day; instead it crashed in an empty field in Pennsylvania. Through phone calls made from the passengers to people on the ground, the passengers found out about what the terrorists had done in New York and Washington, D.C. A passenger named Linda Gronlund called her sister and told her about their hijacking and that the passengers had voted on a plan to take action.

Living the Law of Attraction

I heard about Todd Beamer, another passenger, saying on the phone that some of the plane's passengers were planning to "jump on" the terrorists. Todd's last audible words were, "Are you guys ready? Let's roll." Yes, Flight 93 didn't make it to its intended target because the brave passengers on that flight found out the mission of the terrorists. With "Let's roll," they saved countless lives as the airliner was made to plummet to the ground instead of into the White House, the Capitol building, or whatever target the terrorists had planned to destroy. Hollywood would have given us feel-good endings by having the airliners miraculously land safely on a Pennsylvania field, Dulles Airport, the Beltway, etc. But this was no movie. This was an attack on the United States of America, planned by a cockroach of a man who used holy books and young kids to support the success of his mission.

I know the passenger response on the other three airliners would have been the same as the passengers on United 93 if they had known the hijackings were terrorist missions of murder.

The airlines were grounded for a few days as the country began trying to figure out what on earth had happened. Surprisingly to me, the events of 9/11 did not affect my willingness to fly in our commercial airliners. But the tragedy did break my heart and the hearts of millions of Americans. Like all Americans, I was haunted by the attack and am still haunted by it today.

What's more, my fear of flying and my refusal to fly emerged again after 9/11. Another airliner flying over New York disintegrated in midair. The tail fell off, the engines fell off, and the plane crashed into the ground. I thought that if our planes were falling apart midair it was a good idea to use the car for long trips once again. I did not think this was another terrorist attack, but I did lose faith in the integrity of the planes.

I knew I was afraid to die in a plane crash, even though I also believed that if I were ever in a plane crash it would be a painless death because I'd be dead long before my brain could send pain signals. However, I was still afraid. I'd say to myself that the pilot and crew didn't want to die in this way any more than I wanted to – but it really didn't work all that well for me.

A few weeks after 9/11, I asked my angels and guides to help me conquer my fear of flying. Within two weeks, I was given the response to my prayer request in a dream. Clearly, this dream was a loud and clear message.

The Dream

I was sitting in an aisle seat in the mid-section of a

Boeing 747. That is where I usually try to sit when I fly. I fly Southwest Airlines and because of their open seating arrangement, you will usually find me on the aisle near the wing. Suddenly, the lights were off and the plane was very dark. I sat there in the dark thinking that this could not be good. Then, without warning, the engines shut off and became silent. The darkness of the plane against the silence was surreal. The moments of darkness and silence seemed to last forever, suspended in time. Then suddenly, the plane pitched and began a slow descent, with the wings at 45 degrees and the plane pitch about the same.

I remember sitting there saying repeatedly to myself, "This is not good." I remember hearing people gasping and saying prayers. I saw the people in the seat across the aisle from me holding each other's hands while sitting straight up in their seats, eyes wide open, jaws clenched.

There were magazines, books, and cups hurling through the plane as it began a straight descent. I remember being belted in my seat, feeling the plane jostling as it dove straight down to the earth. It's funny; I didn't really have too many thoughts during this experience. The event seemed to last forever even though I knew we would all be dead in minutes or even seconds. The interior of the plane was very dark because there was no electricity. Interestingly, no one was yelling or screaming. There were gasps, prayers, and silence. I could see the woman across the aisle from me holding her baby to her breast, kissing the infant on the head and softly singing a lullaby.

I closed my eyes as we plummeted to the ground and then suddenly, I was weightless. I opened my eyes and saw that all of us, passengers and crew, were in the air outside the plane. The plane had crashed into the ground far below us. We could see the plane on the ground. It was smashed into many pieces; luggage was strewn, and part of the plane was in flames. But we stayed suspended in the air. We could see each other and we could see many angels in the air with us. I remember looking at everyone and watching everyone looking at each other. The angels were very large beings. They must have been at least eight feet tall and had large wings. The wings seemed stationary because they did not appear to affect the ability of the angels to fly. And, what the heck, we were all in the sky with them and none of us had any wings! Then the sky opened up in a beautiful sort of way. It almost looked like an opening from a distance coming closer and getting larger with sunshine beaming through. We were not "going to the light"; the light was coming to us! Suddenly, my mother and my grandmother were greeting me. They were smiling with joy and radiating love.

Then abruptly, I awoke. It took a few moments (it seemed longer) to understand that this was a dream and I had been in bed sleeping. It was so real that it took a few moments to shake it off.

Clearly, I was being told that our spirits or souls leave our bodies prior to the actual crash into the earth. And, in addition to there being no pain involved, it actually led to a beautiful and joyful experience. If I had had have my way in those waking moments, I would have immediately returned to the dream and enjoyed the company of those I love who had gone before me. Then, I would be off to the great adventure waiting for me on the other side of the sunshine opening!

Yes, I began flying once again. I still take a light-weight anti-anxiety pill before I fly, but the Makers Mark and the white knuckles have been left in the past.

You may be wondering what angel answers have to do with living a serendipitous life. Simply put: it is comforting to have available to us the help of our guides and our angels. We can all call upon our angels to help us. If you have never read books by Doreen Virtue, I recommend that you do. She is an expert on angels.

Another Angel Event

Recently I was scheduled to fly to Chicago for

work. I arrived at the airport 2½ hours early. When I realized how early I was, I was kicking myself that I didn't sleep for an additional hour. I really didn't need to be there at 8:00 when my plane was leaving at 10:30!

If you read my original book, you know I fly Southwest Airlines if at all possible. I was booked on a Southwest flight to Midway Airport in Chicago. I decided to check my luggage, find a magazine, and hang out while waiting for boarding.

When I got to the Southwest lady at the luggage/ticket counter, she asked for my picture ID and my boarding pass. I handed her my boarding pass and went to take my license out of my wallet. Guess what? No license!! I couldn't believe it! I don't think I have been without my license since the time I first got it, about 300 years ago. (Remember, I was alive in the 60s and 70s.) She told me that Southwest was an airline that would let me board without a picture ID but I would be undergoing a thorough search prior to boarding. I wondered what that thorough search meant – yuk. I certainly understood the security reasons for the thorough search and if I were a passenger who was boarding normally (who didn't lose her picture ID), I would expect nothing less from the airline. Anyway, knowing I had a lot of time before my flight, I returned to my vehicle to search for it, bumper to bumper if necessary, because I just knew my license had to be in it somewhere! This was not a time to "manifest" my license because my license already existed somewhere. This was a time to call upon my angels. I may not have known where my license was but I knew they knew! So, I called on my angels to show me where my license could be found. I did not feel or hear or see any messages, so I tore into my CRV looking for my license. The only picture ID in the vehicle was my state government work ID. I brought that ID to the ticket counter and sheepishly presented it to the same Southwest lady. She told me that the ID was acceptable and I no longer needed to submit to their thorough search.

Needless to say, I was relieved. But I was still very concerned about the whereabouts of my license. Knowing I had already asked my angels to reveal its location, I just thanked them for helping me and I knew the answer would come. I was hoping I'd have my license by the time I was ready to leave Chicago, but I had placed my faith in my angels and, with a "thank you," I let it go.

I boarded the aircraft without incident and enjoyed a smooth flight to Chicago.

After getting off the plane at Midway, I began walking toward the signs directing me to baggage claim. Suddenly, I saw a picture in front of my eyes. At about a 45-degree angle as you look toward the ceiling appeared a three-dimensional picture of my license. I stopped and leaned against the wall so I could take in this information. I saw my license in my desk drawer at work. It was leaning against the front of the top right-hand drawer. I thought to myself, "What on earth is it doing there?" But I felt an immediate sense of relief because someone from work was scheduled to join me in Chicago the next day. I called the work operator and asked for that worker's extension, knowing she would be there to answer it. Sally answered her phone on the first ring. I asked her if she would check my top right-hand desk drawer for my license. Minutes later, Sally returned to the phone and told me that indeed it was in my drawer – standing up leaning against the front. Sally brought my license with her to Chicago the next day and believe me, I have not lost sight of it since!

Living a serendipitous life by plugging into the Universe allows you to live a magical daily life. Being able to call upon your angels can really help when the issue before you has little to do with deliberate creation.

Remember, the Universe gives us many tools to support our daily success. Deliberate creation is just one of those tools.

Chapter 19
Near-Death Experience

I had known Anne for a few years when she related this story to me. She spoke of her experience very matter-of-factly, but I was fascinated. It spoke to me of the miraculous changes that happen when we "let go" in our journey of deliberate creation.

Anne had a near-death experience when she was 12 years old. Actually, it was a real death experience.

At that age, because she had contracted polio, Anne had metal braces on both her legs. It was a warm and beautiful summer day when Anne's family decided to go to the lake. Both she and her older sister were on a boat that morning when her older sister, who did not like Anne, decided to push Anne overboard.

Anne remembered sinking like a stone to the bottom of the lake. She could see the sunshine quickly disappear as she was struggling to swim up to the surface while she was sinking under the weight of the heavy metal braces. Anne remembers panicking and working her arms without success. She held her eye wide open but could see only murky darkness and could feel only very cold water.

When she no longer held any air in her lungs and began to breathe in the water, she stopped struggling. Anne knew she was drowning and she accepted her fate.

However, a miraculous event happened when Anne stopped struggling in that dark water. She said, "As soon as I stopped struggling, the dark brownish water turned to a beautiful emerald green. My eyes were wide open and I saw the water change from being very dark to a beautiful emerald green with very colorful fish swimming all around me." The fish were a rainbow of colors. She watched the colorful fish, the emerald water, and noticed streaks of sunshine beaming and colors dancing.

Anne also noticed that she felt absolutely no pain. She said that she became cold on the inside. Later on, while she was recovering in the hospital, she was informed by her doctor that she had become cold on the inside because her lungs were filled with cold water. Anyway, once she felt the inside of her body getting cold, she drifted off to sleep and soon she lost consciousness. According to her doctor, Anne had drowned.

Someone had seen this incident from shore and did swim out to help. He finally found Anne's lifeless body and brought her to the surface. Thankfully, she had been dead only for minutes. She was revived and spent a month recovering in the hospital. She said the recovery was hard because her lungs had been filled with lake water and they had to be restored. The lung restoration was a very painful experience for her. But Anne tells people that her experience with death was beautiful and painless.

When you are trying to manifest an intention, like Anne, you have to let it go. There cannot be the slightest struggle as you manifest your desires. When Anne ceased to struggle, the water and the fish swimming around her turned from darkness into beautiful colors and Anne experienced peace in her acceptance of letting go.

Anne's experience mirrors our experience when we manifest our intentions. When we cease to struggle, let go, and allow the Universe to deliver – we experience miracles.

The example of Anne might appear to be somewhat extreme, but it really is not. Many of us believe we have let go of our intention, but when we are faced with an emotionally charged issue connected with it, we may react with very strong feelings. This indicates that we have not yet let go in order to allow and we are still hanging on and struggling.

I know someone who had set her intention to attract a specific man into her life. She believed she had done all the steps correctly, including letting go of the outcome in order to allow. She found out that she had not really let go of the outcome when someone repeated a rumor to her that the man she had intended to attract into her life already had a girlfriend. She had a strong emotional reaction (an emotional meltdown) to the news and immediately realized she was unable to let go of the outcome entirely. She then stepped back, analyzed the situation, and changed her intention to allow the Universe to select the correct man to enter into her life. Within three weeks, she met the man she eventually married.

When we place our intention and let go of the outcome, we will not experience a strong emotional reaction if contrary news is delivered to us. If we are able to stop struggling and let go of the outcome, we know the Universe will deliver our intention *or something or someone even better*. The Universe knows what we need and what we need is not always what we think we want. Additionally, once you are able to let go of smaller intentions, you will find it easier to let go of the larger intentions.

"I was once asked why I don't participate in anti-war demonstrations. I said that I will never do that, but as soon as you have a pro-peace rally, I'll be there."
Mother Teresa

ing her on the advice of a co-worker. At that time, I lived about ten miles away from her place of business. I have since moved and now the round trip drive is approximately 120 miles if I want Jeannette to make sense of this hair of mine. Considering the rising price of gasoline, you must wonder why I would continue going to Jeannette with all the additional miles it takes. It's safe to say that Jeannette is much more than a hairdresser. But neither is she a friend I see socially. So, who is this person?

Well, let me first say that Jeannette is a gifted hairdresser. She can take a very boring head and create a more interesting head … but creating interesting and attractive heads is not all that she is about. When I think of Jeannette, the first thing that comes to mind is that she is someone who listens well and laughs often. She always has an amusing story to share about her life and she is always interested to hear about the lives of her clients. Jeannette often tells me about her wonderful husband, Bill. Bill is a hard worker and according to Jeannette, he seems to know how to fix any machine, from cars to boats to the snowmakers that blow snow in the mountains every winter. They live in an area of the state that has a very large lake with several islands of various sizes. They bought land on one of the larger islands. Bill is building an island vacation home for them. (I would be remiss if I did not let you know that Jeannette works very hard beside Bill in the building of their island home – and, remember, she has the scissors and may read this, so Jeannette gets building credit along with Bill.)

Anyway, back to being serious ... Jeannette understands love and the loss of love. Her Dad died not too long ago and his death left an empty place in her heart that will never be filled or forgotten. Jeanette is genuine. She has an incredible sense of humor in addition to a warm and caring heart. Whenever I think of Jeannette between appointments, I smile. How many people cause you to smile? Have you let them know they have earned a place in your heart?

I appreciate Jeannette. Who do you appreciate? My life would be the poorer if Jeannette were not walking my life road with me. Take a moment and think about this. Then, when the names of those very important people come to your mind, take a moment to figure out a way to let them know. Love people now. Please do not wait for funerals to express your love and appreciation. Remember, I lost my Dad when I was 12 years old. I learned at an early age that time could not be trusted. Do yourself a favor and step outside your comfort zone and recognize the people you appreciate or love. Love the people you love here and now. If someone causes you to smile when you think of him or her, then find a way to let that person know that he or she is appreciated.

You might let them know of your appreciation through conversations, doing or asking a favor, or a thoughtful holiday card. Let them know just how important they really are to you. You will never meet anyone who is identical to someone else. While it is true that we are all the same, it is also true that each of us is unique. The people who cause you to smile are in your life only for a period of time. Life flows on. When these special people leave us by moving away, or by the death of the body, no matter how long you have been together, once they are gone it is as though they have been whisked away and the brief moments we had are all we have left. Don't let time elapse without, in some way, showing your appreciation to those people who make a difference in your life.

When you live the Law of Attraction, you live a life guided and decided by love, appreciation, forgiveness, and gratitude.

"You cannot do a kindness too soon, for you never know how soon it will be too late."
Ralph Waldo Emerson

Chapter 21
Lessons from Dag

In chapter 2, I talked about balancing our two worlds. I'd like to mention it again here because it is so important to understand this seemingly contradictory concept.

We, like nature, have a life span. There are certain jobs we need to accomplish when we come into this life. When we are infants, we first learn to crawl. Then we hang onto a piece of furniture or we hold onto the hand of an adult in order to stand for our very first time. Then we fall. We stand up again, eventually taking shaky steps, and fall again. We keep going through this standing/walking lesson of crawling, standing, falling, standing, falling, standing, taking a few steps, falling, standing, and finally walking. We pretty much do this in most of our endeavors through life until we finally allow this human body to expire when it is supposed to expire.

It is nice to know that our spiritual growth does not mirror our physical growth. We can grow spiritually in leaps and bounds, but first we must have the courage to leap into the unknown when we get to that precipice that invites us to grow spiritually by self-surrender. We must surrender the temptation to "make things work" when we are practicing deliberate creation. We must take that leap of trust and faith, believing that because the Law of Attraction is a universal law we learn to use it by the act of "not doing." We need to let go and allow, and at the same time acknowledge that we live with limitation, time, and matter. And we need to realize that we came to this existence with a life purpose, a purpose that may well be in conflict with our ego desires.

Perhaps through the eyes of our ego, we desire to be in financial abundance and live in a multi-million dollar home in Malibu. But suppose our life mission is to live as a high school teacher and mother, learning to balance teaching and parenting with the intended outcome of teaching both our students and our children a higher purpose in life. Then what? We are in conflict, between the ego's deliberate intention and our life mission. That is why we have to let go of the ego so our intentions are in line with our mission.

Living in both worlds is very challenging. I am not saying that the teacher in the last paragraph cannot have it all. But I am saying that she has a mission to accomplish as well. We need courage to embrace this adventure. The Universe (God) does want us to have all good things, just as you want your children to have all good things. And you know that as your children grow their choices of "good things" change. As a child, consuming a bowl of Gummi Bears may be, in your child's view, a good thing. You, as the parent, have to make higher-level decisions for your child. The parent is looking at long-term health and happiness for the child, while the child is looking to the current desire. We have all witnessed toddler tantrums. When we first find out about the Law of Attraction, some of us have toddler tantrums when the Universe does not deliver our desired outcome immediately. Others of us find ourselves frustrated, depressed, or maybe even angry. What do we do? Many people keep buying more and more books, CDs, and DVDs, hoping to find the missing answers. We attend lectures, go on cruises, explore websites, read the inspirational messages in our email each day, and on and on.

The positive results we get when we read the numerous books on deliberate creation and when we listen to CDs and attend lectures is that we truly learn the basics and we learn we are more than just a body. We learn that we are loved, that we are creative, and we learn that we can be, do, or have anything.

The not-so-positive results are that when we try and try and try to manifest huge amounts of money, a life partner, a new home, etc., through our ego desires, we get depressed when it's not working.

Most of the Law of Attraction students manifest little things each day. Many of us are used to getting prime parking spaces whenever we need to park somewhere in our shopping/work/appointment travels. We live this serendipitous life because we live from spirit instead of from ego.

As we live from spirit instead of ego, our heart's desires begin to change from the multi- million dollar house in Malibu to deeper, happier, and more joyous experiences. We begin to live from love and our desires change from "Gimmie" to "How can I learn to give and receive love?" We become wealthy in our happiness and in our joy.

Can we still have that house in Malibu? Sure, why not! But you have to learn to crawl before you run marathons.

Just keep in mind what was said in chapter 2: "Because we take part in and agree to the decision about the limitations and challenges we will experience in this lifetime. We even take part in and agree to the decisions about who are parents are, what our socioeconomic status is, and where on this earth we will live. So it is reasonable that we take complete responsibility for what we do with our lives and take responsibility for what we do with our power." Do I believe we can have it all? YES. But, unlike McDonald's, the world is not a drive-up window and we need to wean ourselves off the expectation of instant gratification. The Universe is not a slot machine nor is it an on-demand ATM of desires. The Universe is Source Energy, God, and is an extension of ourselves. We, however, are not God. Just like a branch cannot claim to be the tree nor can the drop of water claim to be the ocean – although we are an extension of God by the power within each of us, we are not God. So we must trust the Universe with our hearts and our minds.

It is really difficult to trust the Universe in this way, but we must. We must trust it to the point that when it seems we are refused our intention, that we accept that the Universe knows best and will deliver our heart's desires when we are ready to receive them. It is in this level of trust that we are truly able to let go of the outcome and see our intentions made manifest.

Dag Hammarskjöld was the Secretary-General of

the United Nations. He was a very accomplished man, who died in a plane crash while on a peace mission in the Congo in 1961.

Mr. Hammarskjöld left behind a diary he had been writing for some years. The diary did not mention his accomplishments in his lifetime. His diary was really a record of his spiritual development – his spiritual awakening.

His diary, *Markings*, was published in 1964. His book caused a profound change in countless lives. Because his book challenged me to be my best and highest self, I would like to share a few of Mr. Hammarskjöld's thoughts with you.

An effective illustration of "letting go" and "allowing" is captured in his quote below:

"Really, nothing was easier than to step from one rope ladder to the other – over the chasm. But, in your dream, you failed, because the thought occurred to you that you might possibly fall."

Often we fail because we have doubt and believe we may fall. For example, this may come through in us by a false belief that we are unworthy. We might think that because we smoke cigarettes or we are 50 pounds overweight that we will not be "worthy" until we stop smoking or lose the weight. Perhaps when we were children, adults who were supposed to love us may have said words to us or about us that caused us to feel we were unworthy. The quote from Dag Hammarskjöld describing the experience of failure due to self-doubt reminds us just how painful our false beliefs really are. When we rid ourselves of false or limiting beliefs, we realize we are worthy just as we are and we welcome positive growth into our lives.

Two additional quotes of Mr. Hammarskjöld that made a difference in my view of life are:

"I don't know Who – or what – put the question, I don't know when it was put. I don't even remember answering. But at some moment I did answer Yes to Someone – or Something – and from that hour I was certain that existence is meaningful and that, there-fore, my life, in self-surrender, had a goal. From that moment I have known what it means 'not to look back' and 'To take no thought for the morrow.'

and

"Never, for the sake of peace and quiet, deny your own experience or convictions."

As you "step from one rope ladder to another" you are giving up your mental limitations and letting go of placing the house in Malibu as your most impor-tant intention. Instead, you are in the process of checking your ego at the door and taking it from the seat of control over your life. Living the Law of Attraction demands that you be not only a better person, but that you be the best person possible – giving the best of yourself every day. There are some days that the best of yourself may be holding your tongue when you feel anger rising and ready to spill out of your mouth. But, when that is your best – then hey, that is your best!

Sometimes your best is simply not criticizing when you are tempted to tell your significant other that dinner was less than wonderful, as you tasted your undercooked salmon. And then, sometimes you really shine!

Chapter 22
Challenges and Joys

When you live a serendipitous life, you get used to miracles happening. Sometimes your deliberate intention appears seemingly out of the blue and sometimes your deliberate creation may take weeks or months. It could be a roll of duct tape or a million dollars – there is really no difference between the two when we speak of the "miracles" that come to us through the quantum field.

As we experience more and more serendipity, we just naturally expect this life to work on our behalf and we vibrate higher and higher. You don't need to raise your vibration when you live the Law of

Living the Law of Attraction

Attraction. Having found the kingdom of God and having plugged into Source Energy and living the Law of Attraction creates consistency in your results. Yes, sometimes you can hit a brick wall in your path so you have to consider if this detour is temporary or permanent. We do not carry all knowledge with us on our journey; thus we look to the Universe for guidance with faith and trust.

We come to this life with challenges to face. Our challenges are in our lives for our learning and growth. If one of your life lessons is to allow someone to minister to you, you may have chosen to endure a long illness in order for a specific someone to care lovingly for you and perhaps be propelled into medical school....or to learn to care, period. If one of your lessons is to learn forgiveness, you will need someone to harm you in some way so that you can learn to forgive.

Not everyone has agreed to be financially abundant or wealthy in this life. If we know we're living our life's purpose, then perhaps we won't want (or feel like we need) some of the superficial things anymore. But our creative ability will cause a less than wealthy life to be full of "coincidences" that meet and exceed our needs and fill us with joy. No matter what we have come to learn and to experience, we can live a life of serendipity and experience the depth and heights of joy.

Challenges and Joys

When I think about living in Third World countries without clean water, without electricity, without wide-screen televisions and a car in the driveway, I think of Carolyn Myss and her work, detailed in her book *Sacred Contracts*. She teaches that we made a sacred contract when we came to this life. But no matter what the contract, it does not preclude a happy serendipitous life no matter what life choice and lessons we have agreed to experience. Viktor Frankl's book on logotherapy says that he was in a concentration camp and he found that the only thing we can control is our reaction to what happens to us. Please do not dismiss this too quickly. If we can control our reaction to what happens to us – even while living in a concentration camp - we realize we actually have the ability "let go" and "allow."

In order to learn to grow and become our higher selves, any life choice that we make will have its learning challenges. Some of us struggle with health issues. Some of us struggle with relationship issues. Some of us struggle with financial issues. We may think that movie stars or Wall Street giants have easy, happy lives because they live a posh lifestyle, but until you are walking in another's shoes, you really don't know that person's life experience.

If someone has what we do not have, we think they must be happy. But we really do not know how anyone else is experiencing life.

Living the Law of Attraction

Many of us believed that Michael Landon (of "Little House on the Prairie," Little Joe Cartwright of "Bonanza") had a miraculous life. We (the public) knew he was handsome, wealthy, and that he had a contagious laugh. However, at age 54 Michael died from cancer; he lived a short life. He had had a very stressful childhood, but according to reading I have done, during his life he "made people feel safe." My feeling is that he is a man who fulfilled his mission and had "it all." He grew through his childhood challenges and grew into a man who made a difference in the lives of those he touched, both in his personal life and on the television screen.

But don't be deceived into thinking that a person should be followed because he seems to "have it all" because of his or her electric personality and large following. Always consider the fruits of the tree.

Michael Landon made people feel safe and his actions told us volumes. He always took time for the young stars on "Little House on the Prairie," protecting them from little star fears. He was generous and he had no need to have control over others. (Control over his business, yes. Control over others, no.)

On an unhappy note, other people — like Hitler and Jim Jones — eventually lead others to destruction, while making them feel safe by controlling their lives. Hitler and Jones had large followings. People responded to their promises with abandon. Jones led his following out of the country and built Jonestown in South America. When his world was beginning to collapse, Mr. Jones gave his flock poisoned Kool-Aid and then shot himself. When Hitler's world was collapsing around him, he shot himself – after having murdered millions of innocent people. Remember, at one point in their lives, these "leaders" gained the trust of many, only to lead every one of them to a course of destruction.

Outer trappings do not always reflect reality. If you are living the Law of Attraction by living through spirit, you will be able to discern the truth from lies. The saying "Listen to your gut" should be heeded. Your gut – or your voice within – will help you navigate through the fruits of the tree so you will be able to stay on your path without any permanent or fatal distractions.

"Those who love deeply never grow old; they may die of old age, but they die young."
A.W. Pinero

Chapter 23
Live Deliberately

"Our deepest fear is not that we are inadequate. Our deepest fear is that we are powerful beyond measure. It is our light, not our darkness that most frightens us. We ask ourselves, who am I to be brilliant, gorgeous, talented, fabulous? Actually, who are you *not* to be? You are a child of God. Your playing small does not serve the world. There is nothing enlightened about shrinking so that other people won't feel insecure around you. We are all meant to shine, as children do. We were born to make manifest the glory of God that is within us. It's not just in some of us; it's in everyone. And as we let our own light shine, we unconsciously give other people permission to do the same. As we are liberated from our own fear, our presence automatically liberates others."

Marianne Williamson
*A Return to Love: Reflections on the Principles of
"A Course in Miracles"*

One aspect of living deliberately is controlling your thoughts. If you do not control your thoughts, you will not be able to manifest deliberately. If something you perceive as being negative happens to you ... oh I don't know ... maybe someone not only cut you off in traffic but in doing so caused you to swerve and lose control of your vehicle for a long moment. Maybe your mother-in-law just insulted your parenting skills. Whatever the situation, the result is you are angry or hurt. These are low vibrational feelings.

First you need to control your thoughts because if you do not then they are off to the races! In the traffic situation, you may be thinking about the "jerk that deserves to have his face punched right through the back of his head." But the more you think about "the jerk," the deeper you dive into negative emotional territory. And you believe that you deserve to lose your temper because you could be dead by now, having had an accident caused by the "jerk"! But even though these thoughts and emotions are completely understandable, they are not serving you at all.

Live Deliberately

You must select thoughts and feelings that serve your best interests. You actually do not know why that person acted the way he or she did. We all have a tendency to move swiftly to judgment, but in order to live deliberately we need to exert control over our thoughts and feelings and withhold judgment.

Years ago, I read a story in *Reader's Digest*. A man and his three small children were on a plane. His children were pretty much running wild and annoying many of the passengers nearby while his nose was buried in a newspaper. After ten or fifteen minutes passed, the father had still not taken control of his children. To the passengers' relief, one irritated person stepped forward and spoke to the man, asking him to be responsible for his children's behavior.

The father, somewhat shaken, apologized for the disturbance. He explained he had just buried his young wife, and he and his children were on their way to his parents' house in a different state. He had been missing his wife and his children were missing their mother and they were acting out their grief in their own ways. It was obvious he felt bad that he had not even noticed his children annoying other passengers.

Having heard this man's story, the passengers quickly took responsibility for the children by reading them stories, talking to them, and entertaining them. They realized the man was grieving so they responded in love. We should learn to respond in love without having to first know the story behind the situation. We need to reach out to each other and believe the best of each other.

This story in *Reader's Digest* has helped me think before I pass judgment. I am sure there are many other stories we have all heard or read about that run along these same lines. It just so happens that this story is the one that made the difference to me and my habit of rushing to judgment.

And, when it comes right down to it – controlling my thoughts and emotions are far more important than enjoying self-righteous anger that does not serve me at all (even though it sometimes feels great for a moment).

The person in the car could have cut you off just because he or she really is a jerk, or he or she could be trying to reach a hospital and worried about a loved one. It really doesn't matter why the incident happened. What matters is that you stay in control of your own thoughts and feelings. Be centered on creating your own reality and allow others to do the same.

Living deliberately also applies to passive behaviors. Let's say you have set your intention to

Live Deliberately

earn an additional $20,000 this year. That is a reasonable deliberate creation.

However, if you spend your week working 40 hours and then you come home to flop on the couch and watch television until you go to bed, you are wasting many hours passively in front of the television. You could be spending at least part of that time working on your goals.

Living deliberately includes where you place your intention. Your attention will wander all over creation if you do not take control of it and redirect it to where you have determined that it should be. Decide where you want to put your intention each day and focus your attention on those areas, typically the areas where you want to see results. Limit the areas where you find yourself wasting your attention.

For example, if your attention is on office cooler conversation and email jokes, your intention is not set on your deliberate creation. You need to control your attention in order to have powerful intentions. Put a sticky note on your monitor with a word that reminds you of your intention – so, instead of gossip and jokes, you think about love, joy, and gratitude.

This comes far more naturally if you have sought and found the kingdom of God within and plugged into Source Energy. However, it is much more difficult, if not impossible, if you have decided to allow your ego to be in the driver's seat, instead of Spirit.

Chapter 24
Goals and Deliberate Creation

There is a difference between goals and deliberate creation. Both goals and deliberate creation are essential to your successful and serendipitous life.

Goals

Goals are what you set in life to accomplish whatever it is you'd like to achieve. If your goal is to become a lawyer, you need to prepare for, apply to, and attend law school. You may go to a four-year school or you may be attending part-time night classes.

Living the Law of Attraction

If you think you might like to sell real estate some day, you need to set that goal. When you set that goal, you then need to find out exactly what it entails. You will need to pass your state real estate exam. You may want to couple that with getting a Notary Public or Justice of the Peace authority. If so, you need to find out exactly where to find the application, how to fill it out, etc. When you set goals, you list objectives. With every objective you meet, it brings you nearer to your goal.

If selling real estate is a goal, one objective may be to sign up for a real estate class. Another objective may be to save the money for the cost of the class. Another objective may be to take the real estate exam. Another objective may be to set up interviews with brokers in your area.

The point is that when you are moving toward a goal, you are creating action lists in order to take logical steps toward that goal. When operating with goals, you are in complete control and you must provide every action as you step toward reaching your goal. In the example of the real estate goal, your deliberate creation activity would come into play when you are interviewing real estate brokers as you apply for a position in their agency. It is then you may want to engage in deliberate creation, in order to get the job in the agency where you will realize your best and highest good.

Goals and Deliberate Creation

Back-planning is an excellent method of planning your goal achievement. Here's how it works.

The first step in your journey is to take the time for concrete study connected to your goal or desire. You need to know exactly what you must achieve in order to get to where you want to be. In addition to any reading you do during your research period, you need to interview people who are already doing the job you believe you'd like to do. Most folks will be happy to tell you whatever you need to know about the business. They will also be able to enlighten you about possible pitfalls, mistakes they made when starting out, and more.

After you have gathered your information, you are ready to back-plan. Your first step is to sit down at a table with pencil and paper. On your paper, create a table using five (or more) columns. When you back-plan, you begin with the end in mind. The "end in mind" here is your goal or your endpoint. Using the example of selling real estate, first you need to decide if you want to sell residential or commercial real estate. Once you feel comfortable with your final goal, you then enter "working for a broker selling real estate by _____" in the fifth or last column. *Include a date.* Make your date of completion reasonable so you are able to achieve your goal on time. (If, down the road, you find you have placed your end date too near or too far off, you can change it, of course. But you will find it easier to meet your goals if you stick to the dates you originally set. You will certainly find it more rewarding and more fulfilling doing it this way.)

Next, in the fourth column you write the last objective you would have to meet in order to complete the goal by the date you selected. In this case, it would be interviewing and being hired to sell real estate for an agency. Again, include a date of accomplishment.

Next, in the third column you would write the second to the last objective you would have to meet in order to move on to column four. In this case, it would be passing your real estate exam. Again, include a date of accomplishment.

Then, in the second column you would write the third to the last objective that you would have to meet before going on to column three. In the second column you write "taking a real estate class or course." And, again, put in a date of accomplishment.

Lastly you would fill in the first column. In that column you write that you will be signed up for your real estate class, with your date of accomplishment.

When you back-plan you place your goal and objectives with their dates of accomplishment. As you move through your written plan, you are constantly moving forward and always keeping the goal in your sight. In fact, when you get to the point of being hired by a real estate agency, you may be expanding your plan. You may create columns that will bring you to the end result of being the broker of your own real estate business with several sales agents working for you.

So, once you accomplish your goal it is time to set another goal! Remember, you are responsible for working your goals. Goal achievement requires work, thoughtfulness, and strategic planning.

Deliberate Creation

Deliberate creation is about *attracting opportunities* into your life. Deliberate creation can help you to meet your goals – but in deliberate creation, you do not need to have a long-term goal as you would if you wanted to sell real estate. If your deliberate creation is to attract an additional $10,000 within the coming six months, then you must work with the Law of Attraction and anticipate opportunities to be attracted into your life with no effort on your part. Your only effort is to *respond* to the opportunities the Universe will bring to you. (This means you will need to get off the couch and respond to the opportunities.) Attracting additional income is very reasonable as you engage the Law of Attraction.

What you do "now" will determine what your

"now" will look like a year from today.

You need to take action to manifest goals.

Some would have you believe that living the Law of Attraction is magic. The Law of Attraction is not done by magical powers creating something from nothing. The Law of Attraction works to draw opportunities toward you so you can act on them. *But it is true that as you experience success in your deliberate creations, your creations will come to you more quickly and easily than in the beginning of your journey.* However, no matter where you are in your journey, you will have to act in order to create. BUT you have to act on inspiration and not act in such a way that you feel you are forcing the deliberate creation to appear. When working with the Law of Attraction, you do not determine how or when the Universe will deliver your intention to you.

You need to trust the Universe to send you the ideas for opportunities for you to act upon. You need to allow the Universe to deliver opportunities to you without boxing out any of the avenues that may be available but are beyond your current knowledge. If you need a new car, do not be looking solely to the Universe to deliver cash to your life. Your opportunity may appear in a drawing for a car, in a gift of a car, a higher-paying position to afford a new car ... who knows? So, when placing your intention, leave the method of outcome to the Universe. Your

Goals and Deliberate Creation

job is to watch for the signs and opportunities.

For example, if your intention is to find a life partner, the opportunity may come through a friend who mentions that a dance class is starting and there are still openings available. If that kind of serendipity happens to you and you feel a small "wow," you should act on the opportunity. However, do not get up each morning contemplating and planning ways you can arrange to meet this person. Can you see the difference?

Make a commitment to yourself to work on your goals and also to be anticipating opportunities the Universe sends to you about your deliberate intentions. But do not confuse goals and deliberate creation.

Realize there is an enormous difference between goals and deliberate creation. In goal setting, you develop your own strategic plan, set your goal, develop objectives and timelines, and provide action in every step of the process. You are in control of your activities and outcomes.

In deliberate creation, you allow the Universe to respond to your intention and only act when you are inspired to do so. In deliberate creation, the Universe will provide opportunities.

You need to balance goal setting and manifesting because you live straddling two worlds.

201

Chapter 25
One Confusing Consideration

As you know, limiting beliefs, unforgiveness, and the like all cause energy blockages in your energy system. When you are having difficulty trying to manifest a heart's desire, there is usually some kind of energy blockage involved that is causing your difficulty.

If you are withholding forgiveness from another person, whether that person is living or has transitioned to the other side, your energy will be blocked and manifesting your heart's desires will be difficult because you are holding on to self-destructive emotions.

Living the Law of Attraction

A reason you really need to pay attention to energy blocks is that the Universe will respond to the energy block *before* responding to your intention. In other words, the Universe will send you opportunities to heal before sending opportunities to act on your deliberate creation. These opportunities to heal may be packaged in meeting someone who reminds you of that unforgiven person, meeting your future son-in-law and he reminds you of that unforgiven person, or a completely different situation or event that mirrors or reminds you of your prior experience. The Universe does all this so you find a way to grow from this experience in forgiveness and love.

The love I am speaking of is not an emotional love. The love I am speaking of is a choice and involves action.

It is easy to act with love toward the people we like and those we love. It is not so easy to act with love toward people who give us the creeps or people we just do not like. That is why love is a choice. If we relied on our emotions or feelings, we would never be able to reach out to the people we have learned to dislike. Sometimes, we dislike someone and we have no idea why we feel the way we do. Sometimes we know it is due to something we learned while growing up, because we remember hateful speech or crass jokes aimed at a certain culture, lifestyle, body type or something else.

One Confusing Consideration

Sometimes we just have no idea at all why it is that we turn from others who have never intentionally harmed us. But the bottom line is that we need to make the choice to act out of love. We have to make the choice of living each day from our higher self.

Again, choosing love is not trying to generate a feeling or an emotional response. When we have discovered and embraced the kingdom within, it requires very little if any effort to be polite and helpful to someone you dislike.

If you are having difficulty forgiving someone or deciding to choose love in response to someone, then the Orange Juice exercise will move you from the state of being unloving to a place of being able to choose love and to be able to forgive. Focus your power with love, gratitude, and forgiveness. It is very important that you are able to remove anything that blocks any of your energy flow.

I realize that some readers have been just about broken in half because they were abused by loved ones. You may be left in shock and despair when your spouse tells you that the marriage is over and a divorce has been filed; or the memories of your childhood consist of constant beatings (or worse) by the very people you love and who are supposed to protect you; or you live with an all-too-familiar barrage of criticism you receive daily and have received daily pretty much from your first memories. If you have been hurt deeply, it may be too difficult for you to forgive your "enemies."

If you have been harmed to such a degree that you are stuck in unforgiveness and you cannot move out of that place, then you might want to consider hypnosis and/or traditional counseling. You must do whatever it takes to allow the kingdom of God to emerge in your life so you are able to plug into that energy and you are able to forgive, remove energy blocks, and manifest your heart's desires. The forgiveness you give to others actually benefits you in many more ways than withholding forgiveness ever will.

When you allow the kingdom of God to emerge in your life, the light of the Universe will shine into those heart places filled with darkness – and as you know, if you walk into a dark room and turn on the light in that room, the darkness disappears. Darkness can never cause light to disappear. Light is powerful. Remember, God created light on the third day, long before he created the sun and the moon. That Light – that kingdom of God - is waiting inside you. This powerful kingdom of God within will only emerge if sought and asked. This kingdom of God is not a bully within us. Rather, this powerful force waiting to be unleashed in our lives will stay still and quiet as it waits for us to seek it out.

One Confusing Consideration

It is imperative that each of us learn to forgive, to live in gratitude, and to make love our decision. As was said earlier, if we remain blocked, our deliberate creations will take longer than necessary because the Universe will send us opportunities to heal in order to remove our blocks and allow our energy to flow freely. Because the Universe knows no passage of time, this process can take minutes, days, weeks, months or years … until such time as we accept our opportunities to heal. When we heal, blockages fall away and our energy flows freely.

When we live a serendipitous life, the Universe works with us and everything seems to work on our behalf. This can only be done by unleashing the kingdom of God within and connecting with Source Energy.

Chapter 26
Living a Serendipitous Life

Serendipity is defined as the ability to make fortunate discoveries accidentally. I take some license with this term. For me, living a serendipitous life means that I live a life of positive coincidences (although I do not believe in coincidence). So, boiled down, living a serendipitous life is living a life where good fortune is always walking beside me. When a downturn happens in my life, the end result is always pretty wonderful. Some examples I mentioned earlier are the tire story and the calendar story.

Another way of describing a serendipitous life is it means to live "lucky." I am actually surprised when

Living the Law of Attraction

I drive somewhere and a convenient parking space is not waiting for me. It is everyday normal life to have convenient parking spaces waiting for me, regardless of the demand for spaces in that particular area.

When I would like to increase my income, opportunities present themselves. All I need to do is to follow up on the opportunities. As an example, I decided I'd like to increase my income this year by another $20,000. As a result of my intention, opportunities to instruct online and in the classroom have been landing in my lap and I was promoted at work.

Just the opposite can occur as well. Several months ago I decided that I'd like to take time off from teaching. Soon thereafter I was contacted by the university and told very apologetically that classes fitting my areas of study were not being offered that semester. How wonderful was that!! I had been feeling hesitant and awkward about calling to bag the next semester. Now, it was done for me! The refreshing rest I received while away from teaching for that semester was just what I needed.

Living a serendipitous life is a wonderful walk in this life. I always expect the best opportunities and outcomes.

It is true that you will meet people who will want to rain on the parade of your lucky life. When you encounter these folks, just forgive them with love and keep walking your walk. I for one cannot understand the hatefulness or meanness of some people on this earth. I cannot understand or accept hateful behavior resulting in harm to others. Why do some people commit child atrocities? Why do some people abuse or take financial advantage of the elderly? Why do some people abuse animals? Why does any nation declare war on another? These are examples of behaviors I truly do not understand – nor do I want to understand them. However, I know that the people who commit such horrific acts or who make such destructive decisions have not genuinely sought the kingdom within and made a decision to live in that kind of servant-leadership role – a service to others and a leader by example. No, I will never understand people who appear to thrive on cruelty but I do not despise them. Sometimes the best you can do is to say a quick prayer for them. If you are wondering if I would turn a person in to the police who was causing harm to a person or animal – wonder no further. I would turn them in in a heartbeat. Remember, we live straddling two worlds and we have to live in balance. I come from a justice background and I firmly believe in community safety and accountability, as well as rehabilitation.

So, living a serendipitous life is both a wonderful way to live and it is a life of responsibility to others. We are charged with treating each other as we would like to be treated. At time, the choice to love is not as easy as it sounds, but I wouldn't have it any other way!

You may be asking: if living the Law of Attraction is not as easy as it sounds, why do it? In addition to everything else I have shared about the subject, I'd like to draw your attention to the core of this life.

Yes, the choice to love is powerful and it can bring you happiness and freedom every single day of your life. You not only look at life differently, you actually experience life differently. You experience everything in your life as part of you. As you breathe in the crisp fall air, you fully know and understand your connection with the Universe and all life around and inside of you. You are one with everyone and everyone is one with you. We all share the same energy and we have a variety of ways we experience our search for our ultimate selves. We see grace in others as well as in ourselves. It is natural to forgive and it is natural to embrace.

Others only appear to be different. Everyone is unique and is living a unique life - but at the same time, everyone is sharing oneness with all creation. The degree to which a person feels separate and alone is the degree to which that person is not walking in love or sharing the experience of a serendipitous life.

Love yourself just as you are, right this very moment.

Living a Serendipitous Life

Love yourself with all the faults and warts. Love everyone else with all their faults and warts as well. As we walk our spiritual journey, the warts and faults pale in comparison to the world love opens for us.

Practice unconditional love by the act of giving without expecting anything in return.

"Barrington Bunny" is a story in a book by Martin Bell, published in 1970, titled *The Way of the Wolf*. I suggest you buy this book and read all its wonderful stories. I recommend this book to anyone seeking a fullness of spiritual life.

The story about Barrington tells of a bunny who feels very alone. He believes that he has no special gifts and nothing to offer anyone. But he discovers that he does have gifts, and that all the animals in the forest are his family. And he learns to love.

All the people on this earth (and I place pets into this category as well – but that's just me) – at least our section of this earth - are members of our family.

I have a friend named Joan. She and her husband retired to the Cape eight years ago. Joan is a wonderful person who understands that all the people in her life are members of her family.

You may be thinking that it's easy for someone who's comfortably retired, able to live however she wants, to believe that all the people in her world are members of her family.

Joan worked her entire adult life in child protection. She lived in several states through the years, but the profession of child protection was always a constant in her life. Joan was consistently promoted to leadership positions throughout her career. She dealt with absolutely horrific child abuse and neglect situations for thirty years. She dealt with situations where children either died at the hands of, or were killed directly by, their caretakers. Joan discovered babies in the state of "failure to thrive" (a state where all major organs are breaking down and slowly dying) because they were left in dresser drawers for days at a time while their parents were out doing heroin or crack cocaine. She held major inquiries into the deaths of many children and had to become intimately involved, through file reviews, interviews, and pictures of the dead or dying children, in order to thoroughly understand the situations.

It is fair to say that Joan has seen the dark side of life day after day for many, many years. Many people would become jaded and lose faith in strangers around her. Not in this case!

She is the mother of two successful sons. One is an entrepreneur who acts in television movies as well as being a stock market trader and having other businesses. The other holds an upper management position at one of our Ivy League schools. Joan's wonderful husband is a veteran from World War II and a retired businessman. She has two remarkable grandchildren. Joan could just relax and enjoy her retired life after thirty years of the daily heartbreak and frustration she experienced in her professional life. (She celebrated success during those years as well –the success of keeping children safe.)

In addition to the "grandmother routines" (babysitting, school duty, etc.), since the day Joan retired she has been volunteering at local shops and libraries each week without skipping a beat. She has reviewed child abuse cases for other states and has given guidance. And, every morning, Joan takes a walk and calls it her paper route. She goes to the homes of all the elderly in her neighborhood, picking up the newspapers thrown to the end of the driveways and placing them on the porches within easy reaching distance for the folks who would have had difficulty getting those newspapers from the driveway.

Joan has always responded to the needs of the folks in her part of this world. She is a good friend to anyone who needs her.

Joan "gets it." She knows we are all on earth to help each other and that each of us has unique gifts we bring to this world. Joan knows that "all the animals in the forest are members of her family." Joan will love you with food (she is a wonderful cook) and regale you with wildly funny stories (like the time a state police helicopter swooped down to hover over her car – the police officer shouting though his loudspeaker for her to slow down! She was driving though mountain roads and thought she would not get caught with her lead foot.) She will listen to you when things are rough in your life. She will walk beside you, regardless of difficult situations you may be facing.

Her grandchildren will benefit from the opportunity of watching her as she lives her life while she sets an example for them. They will learn all about unconditional love and acceptance.

Do you have any Joans in your life? If you do, it may benefit you to take time to talk with them and spend time with them. Because we live in separate states, I get to see Joan once a year. We talk on the phone once in a while and email often. I count myself lucky for having this person in my life and I do *not* take Joan for granted.

If you know a Joan, do not take that person for granted. That person is living their life purpose!! Learn from them. Come to really understand that "all the animals in the forest are members of your family."

If you are able to embrace this concept, you will live a marvelous life of wonder and appreciation.

Chapter 27
In Closing

My journey was longer than necessary because I really had no one to guide me. I met many wonderful people who had a great deal of knowledge, but that knowledge also included the instruction that "their way was the only way." I just never felt comfortable with that concept because you cannot help but leave out large segments of any population. I believe in inclusivity and reaching out to everyone but I also believe that people are free to believe whatever best serves them.

A friend once told me, "You have something to give to everyone and everyone has something to give to you." Yes, we are a combination of all we have learned from others along our way in this life. I guess each of us is a patchwork quilt. Each quilt is basically the same and each quilt is uniquely different from the others. We are like that. We are the same and we are uniquely different. Each of us has been given gifts to share with others. Some of us listen, some of us teach, some of us fix, some of us laugh. We all have our gifts we bring into this world.

I am a student of metaphysics but I take the New Testament seriously in that I believe I should live by the teachings of Jesus. Because of the many books of the Bible that were banned, the ancient scrolls that were unearthed, the yet-to-be discovered ancient scrolls, and the destroyed ancient scrolls, it seems to me we may never discover the full richness of the Bible or the teaching of Jesus in our lifetime. It is true that I enjoy the Old Testament, but I follow the teachings of Jesus as best as I can.

For example, "Open letter to Dr. Laura" on the Internet tells me volumes in its own humorous way. In case you have yet to see this document, I Google-searched it and present it now to you for your enjoyment.

In Closing

An open letter to Dr. Laura
J. Kent Ashcraft

May 2000

Dear Dr. Laura,

Thank you for doing so much to educate people regarding God's Law. I have learned a great deal from your show, and I try to share that knowledge with as many people as I can. When someone tries to defend the homosexual lifestyle, for example, I simply remind him that Leviticus 18:22 clearly states it to be an abomination. End of debate.

I do need some advice from you, however, regarding some of the specific laws and how to best follow them.

a. When I burn a bull on the altar as a sacrifice, I know it creates a pleasing odor for the Lord (Lev 1:9). The problem is my neighbors. They claim the odor is not pleasing to them. Should I smite them?

b. I would like to sell my daughter into slavery, as sanctioned in Exodus 21:7. In this day and age, what do you think would be a fair price for her?

c. I know that I am allowed no contact with a woman while she is in her period of menstrual uncleanliness (Lev 15:19-24). The problem is, how do I tell? I have tried asking, but most women take offense.

d. Lev 25:44 states that I may indeed possess slaves, both male and female, provided they are purchased from neighboring nations. A friend of mine claims that this applies to Mexicans, but not Canadians. Can you clarify? Why can't I own Canadians?

e. I have a neighbor who insists on working on the Sabbath. Exodus 35:2 clearly states he should be put to death. Am I morally obligated to kill him myself?

f. A friend of mine feels that even though eating shellfish is an Abomination (Lev 11:10), it is a lesser abomination than homosexuality. I don't agree. Can you settle this?

g. Lev 21:20 states that I may not approach the altar of God if I have a defect in my sight. I have to admit that I wear reading glasses. Does my vision have to be 20/20, or is there some wiggle room here?

h. Most of my male friends get their hair trimmed, including the hair around their temples, even though this is expressly forbidden by Lev 19:27. How should they die?

In Closing

i.　I know from Lev 11:6-8 that touching the skin of a dead pig makes me unclean, but may I still play football if I wear gloves?

j.　My uncle has a farm. He violates Lev 19:19 by planting two different crops in the same field, as does his wife by wearing garments made of two different kinds of thread (cotton/polyester blend). He also tends to curse and blaspheme a lot. Is it really necessary that we go to all the trouble of getting the whole town together to stone them? (Lev 24:10-16). Couldn't we just burn them to death at a private family affair like we do with people who sleep with their in-laws? (Lev. 20:14)

I know you have studied these things extensively, so I am confident you can help.
Thank you again for reminding us that God's word is eternal and unchanging.

Your devoted disciple and adoring fan."

I hope you enjoyed the "Open Letter to Dr. Laura." It makes a few very good points, at least to me. So, I choose to live by the simple teachings of Jesus, leaving out all the complexities of the Old Testament and the "who said what" in the New Testament. In fact, I own a red letter-New Testament, so when I want to find the teachings attributed to Jesus

Living the Law of Attraction

I just look for the red print. Yes, I do live a simple philosophy as I live my life and engage in the magical wonderful life the Universe offers to us. Deliberate creation is our gift, "a free gift with no strings attached" given to us by the divine intelligence and infinite love of the Universe.

Please let me know if I have helped. Let me know if I said something that needs additional clarification.

"Ideas are clean. They soar in the serene supernal. I can take them out and look at them, they fit in books, they lead me down that narrow way. And in the morning they are there. Ideas are straight – But the world is round and a messy mortal is my friend, Come walk with me in the mud….."

Hugh Prather
Notes to Myself
1970

I invite you to contact me at *kmackenzie123@gmail.com*. I'd love to hear from you!

To your best and highest good,
Kathleen